Facing Fear, Finding You

Facing Fear, Finding You

Build Inner Safety and Transform Your Relationship with Fear

The Fear Series: Volume One

I.K. RANDHAWA

Disclaimer

This book is presented to you for informational purposes only and is not a substitute for any kind of professional personal development advice. The content of this book is based solely on the personal views and opinions of the author, should not be considered scientific or correct conclusions, and does not represent the views of others. All information provided here is "as is" and without warranty of any kind, expressed or implied.

Although we strive to provide accurate general information in this book, we do not guarantee that the content is free from any errors or omissions, and you should not rely solely on this information. Always consult a professional in the area for your particular needs and circumstances prior to making any professional, business, legal, and financial or tax-related decisions.

The author of this book is not engaged in the practice of rendering any professional advice. You agree that under no circumstances, the author and/ or our officers, employees, successors, shareholders, joint venture partners, or anyone else working with the author shall be liable for any direct, indirect, incidental, consequential, equitable, special, punitive, exemplary, or any other damages resulting from your use of this book including but not limited to all the content, information, stories, and products presented here.

We may share success stories of other people in this book as examples to motivate you, but it does not serve as a guarantee or promise of any kind for your results and successes if you decide to use the same information and personal development tips offered here. It is your sole responsibility to independently review the content presented here, and any decisions you make and the consequences thereof are your own.

We reserve the right to update the content and information in this book from time to time as needed.

Subscribe

Thank you for buying this book! If you would like to stay up to date with all of my future publications, please scan the QR code below and subscribe to my mailing list by visiting www.ikrandhawa.com.

Table of Contents

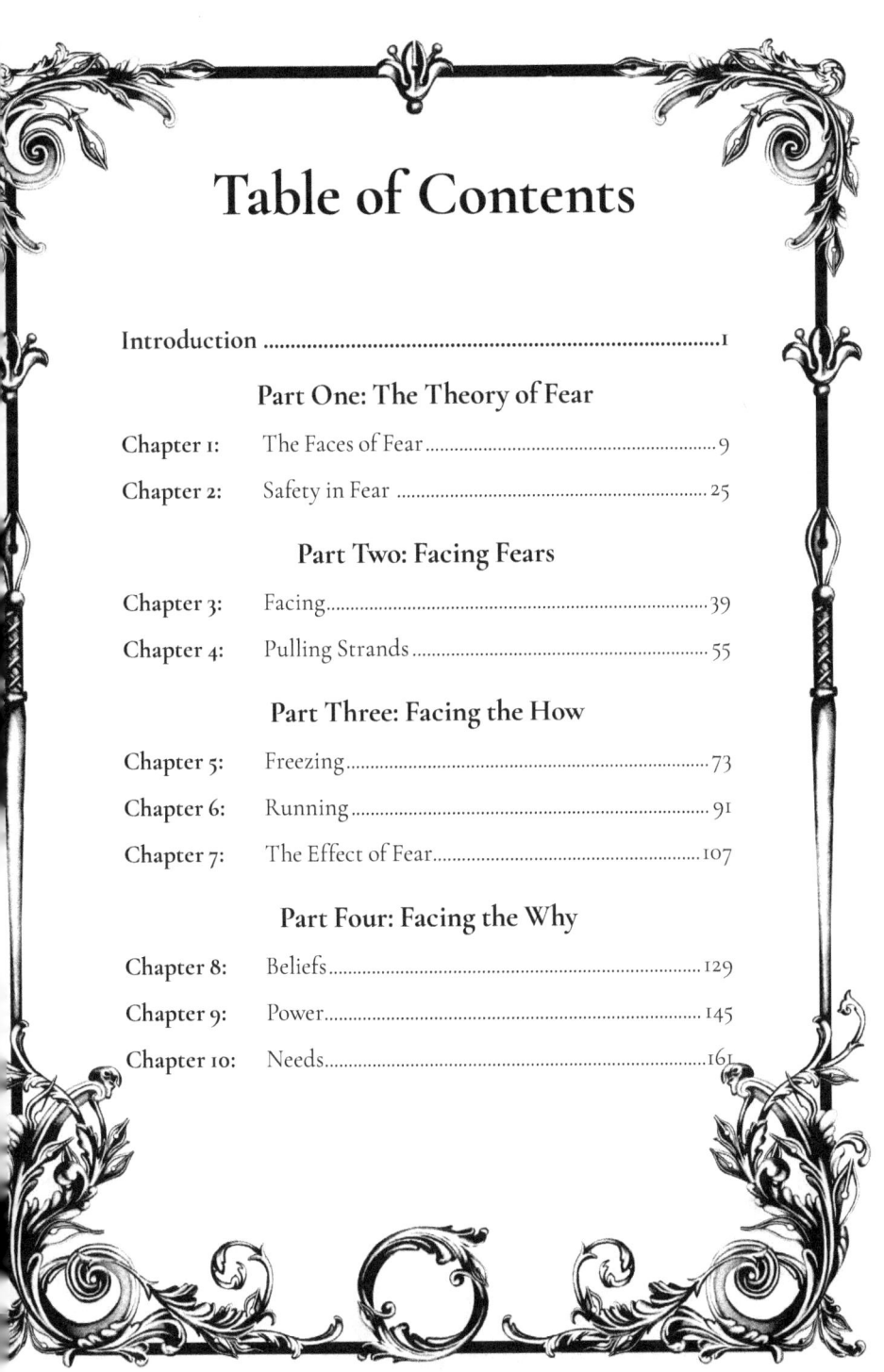

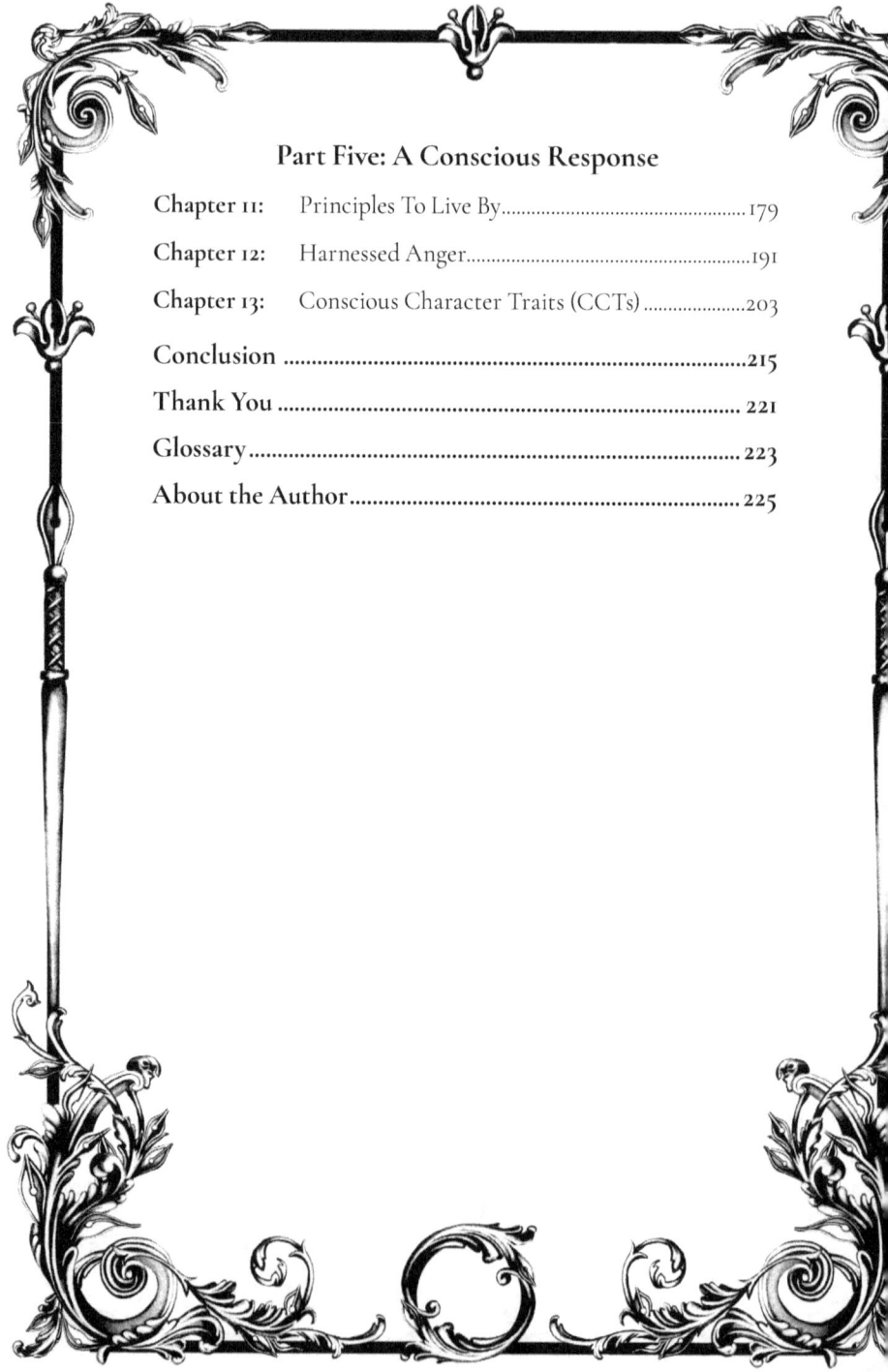

Part Five: A Conscious Response

Introduction

I 'd like to begin by making one thing clear: This is not a fear-fighting book. If you are looking for advice on actions you can take to fight your fears, you won't find it here. That is volume two of the Fear Series, which will thoroughly cover a range of different actions you can learn to harness in your need to become a skilled fear fighter.

However, if you are looking for a book that explores the concept of internal fears, helping you understand how they are sabotaging you on a daily basis, then this book is for you. If you would like to read about some ideas on how you can snap yourself out of anxiety enough to think clearly again, this book is also for you.

Why am I writing a book about facing fears, though? Especially when everyone would rather skip to fighting their fears instead?

Well, the truth is that I started my authorship journey by writing one book on internal fears. I set it out into three parts: The first was the theory behind how internal fears sabotage us; the second was action-based fears; and the third was socially active fears.

But after I finished my rough draft, I realised each section needed its own book to thoroughly explore the topic. Without doing this, I was cutting corners and missing essential exploration. I wasn't understanding the topic as well as I needed to; therefore, I couldn't present a comprehensive product for you.

I understand most people would rather read one book that covers everything. I honestly tried, but I couldn't produce it. There was too much to explore. Therefore, if the fear-facing journey is not of interest to you, then I encourage you to read volume two instead.

Now, for those of you who do want to read this book, let me explain the problem this book addresses. I chose fear as the topic to start my authorship journey because I see too much of it in the world. Everywhere I look, I see people who are afraid.

This hurts me. Too many people are suffering from the permanent pain of harmful internal fear, and it's not pleasant realising we are living in a fearful world. I would like to change this because I used to always be afraid too. Fear of inadequacy is the one that I battled with the most, and I wanted to change the power it had over me.

Thus, on my journey, I realised I had lived my whole life being aware that I was afraid, though I had very limited

2

conscious awareness of what all my fears actually were. That meant I was uninformed and ill-equipped in my pursuit of fighting them.

I had to learn to earn the power of knowledge so I could fight my fears better. Facing and seeing them in their entirety is how I did that. This book can help you to do the same thing. You can learn more about your internal fears, defining exactly what they are and recognising how they are sabotaging you.

You can also learn more about yourself in this process. You see, it took me a long time to realise that in facing my fears, I was actually finding myself. Understanding the true causes of my fears showed me what I believed about myself. About my powers and obligations. My needs. It showed me how I wasn't actively choosing any of my responses and instead was acting out of autopilot.

I found that I hadn't been living as the person I consciously wanted to be. I decided to change that by addressing my biggest opponent: my fears. The ones stopping me from being someone I respect and am proud to be.

When I realised the ways my harmful fears were sabotaging me, I lost all respect for them. The trust I had put in them vanished because they didn't deserve it. They were hurting me, and so they had no place in my mind or life. I chose to value my peace and happiness over my fears and brought myself to a place where I am not constantly suffering in fearful pain anymore.

And when my fears are triggered, I'm able to quickly realise that I'm just feeling afraid and disregard it because I don't give value to that concept anymore. I literally just think, *Oh, I'm just feeling afraid right now,* and shrug it off because I don't respect it enough to keep it.

The thing I have realised is that we don't heal internally like our bodies do. It may be because, physically, we don't ever consciously heal. Our bodies automatically do it for us every day. Whereas, internally, that's not the case. When we experience something traumatic, it hurts us, and we don't immediately start healing the wound. Instead, we mark it as a clear internal danger and fear it because we have chosen to give that pain a high amount of significance.

Imagine if our bodies did the same thing, and after we were bruised one time, we became incredibly afraid of being bruised again. So we lived the rest of our lives never doing anything that could possibly bruise us. It's not exactly the most fulfilling life.

I know you may be thinking that there are different types of pain, and people get hurt every day. That is absolutely true, and your survival and well-being is, at the end of the day, always your responsibility. In my life, I have chosen to believe that my internal fears are a danger in themselves to my well-being.

I would like to assert, however, that you can change your experience of life drastically by being willing to change your position to your internal fears and dangers. You can, and will, become a completely different person. If

that is something you're interested in, then I am honoured to welcome you to reading this book.

Experience

I have reached a point where I am fear-aware and consciously responsive. That's not to say I am completely fearless. I'm not and likely never will be. The decision to become an author has come with its own set of fears I've had to face and overcome.

I'm telling you this because I'm not going to pretend to have all the answers. I am an experienced internal explorer, however, as I have chosen to create this original work purely from my own experiences, intuition, and observations, all without being inspired by or referring to theories by others. That said, I acknowledge that universal truths often echo across different works. Any similarities you may find are simply a reflection of shared experiences.

I do not present any of my thoughts, ideas, and suggestions to you as the absolute truth. Rather, they are thought starters. My hope is that you read what I've written, and then reflect on what resonates with you—and what doesn't. Agree with me. Disagree with me. However you react to this book is a success, because any reaction will bring attention—consciousness even—to your relationship with fear. And in doing so, you'll hopefully grow, as I have.

Metaphors

I have written this book with a mix of personal stories and creative analogies and metaphors I've selected to explain these concepts. This is my preferred way of teaching—always has been. The metaphors are memorable and sometimes funny. I very much enjoy them, and I hope you do too.

I know that my style of writing is not conventional, though, and so you may find the references to the metaphors confusing or overwhelming at times. I have tried to keep them as simple and relevant as possible for you and created a glossary at the back of the book listing out all of the metaphors from the book.

Finally, I hope this book, and all my future works, will help you as much as they helped me. Writing this book challenged and enlightened me. Saved me. Reading it will hopefully ignite a similar journey.

PART ONE
The Theory
of Fear

Chapter One

The Faces of Fear

Fear affects us all—whether you admit it or not. It's woven into the fabric of your life with a weight as constant as your memories and beliefs. And as you grow, fear grows with you. Each new responsibility brings a fresh form of fear—even though you didn't ask for it.

Fear doesn't knock politely or ask for permission. It barges in, tearing down every strength you've built and every piece of wisdom you've collected. You feel it in your body first: racing heart, tightening chest, short breaths. Your muscles tense, bracing for a blow. Your mind spirals, reaching for something—*anything*—to hold on to.

You see, fear makes you vulnerable.

It makes you feel like you're standing bare in the heart of the Arctic. A relentless invasion whispers lies and makes

you believe you're helpless. Your strength, wisdom, and confidence are turned to paper-thin glass, ready to shatter with the faintest pressure. It steals your focus, your control, your sense of self.

It's raw and overwhelming. Utterly paralysing.

In short, fear doesn't care about the truth. No matter what you want or who you are, it forces you to live only for survival—even when your survival is not in question.

Ironically, we live in a society where fear is spread widely by the media, and yet on a personal and professional basis, we're expected to live as though it doesn't exist inside of us. I've noticed the widely held belief that if someone is a professional of something—take an athlete like a football player, for instance—that fear should not be something affecting their performance. As if the fact that they're being paid should extinguish all nerves and doubts, when in reality that's not true at all. In actuality, the professional aspect usually increases the pressure to succeed, and thus increases the fear. It also doesn't give the individual the opportunity to thoroughly face and fight their fear, because they can only focus on going from one performance to the next.

Just because we're convinced that fear should be an insignificant or non-existent part of our lives, doesn't mean that it is. It can be quite damning actually, because it takes over everything. Especially when it's an unconscious permanent internal fear.

The Four Faces

Fear is not a singular emotion but a complex mix of sensations and reactions. Sometimes it creeps upon you— slowly suffocating your thoughts and leaving you gasping for air. Other times, it strikes like a bolt of lightning, igniting every nerve in your body with its electric shock. The fears that stem from our deepest insecurities are not the same as those triggered by external threats because their root causes are worlds apart.

How you respond to your fears should be tailored to the type of fear it is and how much you trust the danger it's spotlighting to you. If you respond to all your fears in the same way, in a freeze or run response, you'll never be able to change yourself and your experience of life. Instead, you are trapped because you are blindly trusting information your fears are relaying to you, rather than questioning them.

Therefore, in order to consciously decide which fears deserve your respect for their reliability, I'd like to break down the ways different fears exist, so you understand their various forms.

We will explore how fears take different forms, which I have split into nature (physical and internal) and duration (temporary and permanent). Both physical and internal fears can be temporary and permanent:

Temporary Physical Fears – Active fear is less commonly experienced, such as stumbling on stairs. This is not something that happens on a daily basis.

Permanent Physical Fears – Active fear is common, such as a fear of certain animals or flying. This is more common than temporary physical fears, though is only activated when you come in immediate contact with that danger, such as a barking dog.

Temporary Internal Fears – Less commonly activated, such as fear of being misunderstood by someone in a specific scenario. These are typically resolved quickly, and you don't usually develop a permanent fear from it.

Permanent Internal Fears – Most commonly activated fears, in that the host is permanently being influenced by this fear on a daily basis. Experiences such as negative feedback, single or repeated, create a fear of inadequacy that affects every area of one's life.

Nature

Physical Fears

A physical fear activates from the presence—or even the existence—of a potential physical danger. This type of fear is deeply personal, unique to each individual, and is shaped by what you believe is a threat to your physical well-being. It also depends on your physical risk tolerance and how much significance you give to pain inflicted on your body.

For some, the mere thought of riding a roller coaster is terrifying, while others feel only excitement. Similarly, one person might be afraid of taking drugs because the risks are too dangerous for them, whereas for others it's exhilarating. Physical fear is always tied to something that could damage your body and cause it pain. It stems from a deep love and instinctual need to protect your body and keep it away from what you believe is a danger.

Internal Fears

Whereas, internal fears are born from the presence of a potential danger to your internal self. Whether you believe that to be your mind, soul, or personality is not as significant as knowing that it's the part of you that isn't your body.

Internal fears, therefore, stem from a belief that certain personal or interpersonal concepts or experiences pose a threat to your internal self. They are something that could cause you to experience emotional or mental pain.

While the physical world offers a finite number of things that can be a danger to us, the possibilities for what could harm us internally is limitless. Change. Intimacy. Being alone. Inadequacy. Shame. Judgment. Helplessness. These are just a few of the vast array of internal fears that can trouble someone. Whether you fear something on your own or in connection to others, these fears have a powerful hold over you.

Internal fears are just as real as physical. The experience of them is the same. Your physical instincts choose your physical fears, and your subconscious chooses your internal. It chooses them and holds on to them, often without you even realising it. Regardless of where your fears come from, the only thing that matters is that they exist. They are real fears, held inside of you.

Duration

Temporary Fears

Temporary fears are like gusts of wind—here one minute, gone the next.

They flit by swiftly, leaving only a trace of their presence behind. They appear when an imminent threat looms in front of you. But just as quickly as they came, they leave.

Whether it's almost getting into a car accident, stumbling on stairs, or being misunderstood by someone, these situations all trigger short-term temporary fear within you. In response, your body's cortisol and adrenaline levels surge, preparing you for battle.

You instinctively assess the situation, and gather all the information you need to find an immediate solution, allowing you to take swift action to prevent the feared danger from becoming a reality. Once the situation

is resolved, your fear fades away. Dopamine floods in, bringing with it a sense of relief and gratitude.

These fears possess impressive reflexes, always ready to spring into action at a moment's notice. Their quickness is admirable, and their role in keeping you safe is undeniable. I appreciate temporary fears because they do their job and leave.

But what if your solution isn't successful? What if the threat becomes a reality?

Well, even then, you don't remain in a state of fear. Instead, you shift into problem-solving mode, taking whatever steps are necessary to deal with the situation at hand. The temporary fear may have served its purpose in alerting you to danger, but it doesn't linger. It gives you the space you need to drive your actions in the face of adversity.

Permanent Fears

Permanent fears are a different beast entirely. Examples are your fear of heights, failure, or of being alone.

They cling to you like an unwelcome shadow, attaching themselves onto your very being. Craving control, they mold you into someone who exists around their presence.

These fears are possessive. Unrelenting.

They want to be the reason for your transformation, demanding you shape yourself around their existence.

Temporary fears are easy to handle. They make their appearance known but don't demand more than what is necessary. Permanent fears, on the other hand, are

insatiable for more—more attention, more time, more energy—more power over you.

Permanent fears are like a colony of parasites, burrowing deep into your mind and feeding on your weaknesses and doubts. They manipulate you, whispering lies convincing you that breaking free is impossible and that you cannot exist without them.

Now that we have explored the different types of fears, I encourage you to become aware of their distinctions in your own life and think about how you are responding to them. It's likely that you have grouped all fears together into one experience for yourself, so you don't realise there's a difference between them.

You're probably also trusting them all equally, not thinking to question them and their sources of information.

Unconscious Permanent Internal Fears

From now on, we will only be addressing unconscious permanent internal fears in this book and the rest of the series.

Before we move on to the reason for this, I'd like to make clear the distinction between conscious and unconscious fears. A conscious fear is something you have questioned and knowingly chosen to keep. Whereas an unconscious fear is something you are hosting that you haven't consciously chosen to be afraid of, haven't questioned the reliability of, and are blindly trusting.

Most of your current fears will be unconscious fears. Not all of them are bad. Depending on your experiences,

most may be valid, and you may want to keep them. The point is that you actually need to face and question them enough to decide to either make them conscious or get rid of them.

Therefore, unconscious permanent internal fears are the focus because they are a danger to you.

How can a fear be dangerous, though? Well, as we've explored above, permanent fears are those that exist within you at all times. When combined with being an internal fear, these fears aren't only existing, but they're permanently activated as an internal danger, like the fear of inadequacy. Being afraid of not being good enough does not affect just one area of your life. It might begin in one, but it spreads to others, and maybe even every area of your life, meaning it is permanently activated.

A permanent physical fear, like the fear of dogs, is only activated when you see a dog. Otherwise, you don't walk around afraid of a dog while you're in a known safe space, like your home.

Permanent internal fears weigh you down, dragging you under and consuming your thoughts. Because these fears live within you, they colour everything—your relationships, your decisions, your entire life. Your subconscious becomes obsessed with survival. Every thought and action revolves around protecting yourself from the internal danger.

What makes these fears particularly dangerous is the unconscious part. You are blindly trusting the information a fear gives you about a danger without assessing it for

yourself, and the high significance placed on that danger. By not questioning whether the information is reliable or not, you can't decide whether it deserves the reaction and focus you're giving it.

In a way, the fear is deceiving you. It's making you believe something will cause you terrible internal pain if you experience it. Even when the reality is that it's usually not a real danger to you at all and will rather aid in your growth and happiness. Yes, you may feel a slight sting from the experience, because that's what most growth is, but it's not dangerous.

By believing that it is, though, you are not only living in the constant pain of fear—which, make no mistake, is a painful existence—but when you do experience the "danger," it's amplified by your fearful beliefs.

Take the fear of failure as an example. You can live your whole life being afraid of any and every type of failure, from a "failed" exam to a "failed" relationship. You can make every effort to avoid this danger, amplifying your belief about how experiencing it will be the worst possible pain you could imagine. And yes, there would be some uncomfortableness to experience. But it's not as bad as what you believed it to be. It's not world ending or life ruining. You can navigate from this position, and usually, bring yourself to a better place.

Failure is not something you need to be permanently afraid of. It's not a high-significance danger to you. But you're trusting your fear and believing that it is.

You often blindly trust your fears because your instincts tell you they're showing you what you need to do to survive. But when the fear is alerting you to a danger that is not a real threat, isn't realistically avoidable, and allows you to thrive, the fear is sabotaging you instead. Unconscious permanent internal fears are not trustworthy.

And why would you ever trust something that is sabotaging you and making you live in constant internal fear and pain?

You wouldn't, would you? But you are, and I'll show you how in the following section.

The Black Cat

Imagine yourself walking down a quiet forest path when, suddenly, a sleek black cat appears before you.

You freeze.

Your heart pounds with terror.

You've heard the rumours of the mythical, dangerous black cats. People say they are witches in disguise. You don't know what to do. The rumours never explained much else.

The creature doesn't seem aggressive or angry, but its eyes watch you as it slowly approaches.

You try to move, but your body doesn't respond.

The cat circles around you, examining you from a safe distance. Its gaze feels heavy, assessing you, deciding whether to make you into its next victim.

You lower your eyes as a sign of submission.

After a few minutes, the cat becomes uninterested. It slinks off into the shadows without a second glance.

You let out a shaky breath, making sure it's gone before continuing on your journey with nervous steps—terrified of meeting it again.

The black cat is your internal amplified danger. Something you are afraid of, that in reality, doesn't pose much of a threat to you at all. Sure, it has the potential to scratch or reject you. But any harm will be minimal.

How and why is a danger amplified? Well, you amplify dangers by allowing yourself to focus only on the potential negative consequences of experiencing that "danger," not any positive ones. This means you don't have a balanced or reasonable perspective to base your belief of the severity of the danger. You just believe it is extremely threatening to you and that you need to stay away from it.

The reason for this may be that when we're initially afraid of something, sometimes we look for evidence to support that fear or belief. We may want to keep that fear, and so we will try to find reasons to do that. Whereas, if we don't want to keep it, we will naturally look for opposite evidence to disprove the likelihood of it.

But if you can amplify that danger, you can also mute and disprove it. Learn to not fear it anymore because you've looked at all the evidence. Not just one side of it. And that's what this book is about. Realising that you are afraid of something internally more than you need to be,

and it doesn't pose as big a danger to you as you have been thinking.

Now, you may argue here that the amplified dangers concept also applies to physical fears. Yes, it does. I'm not saying that it doesn't. But those amplified dangers don't frighten you away from peace and growth the way that internal ones do.

I also argue that physical amplified dangers are easier to judge the severity of threat compared to internal ones. Take the fear of dogs as an example. This is an amplified danger that's created a permanent physical fear. When you encounter a dog on the street, you can easily judge the severity of the threat to you based on the size and breed of it, how far away it is from you, and whether it looks like it's about to attack you or not. You can then decide whether you'd like to avoid it or challenge yourself to ask permission to pet it.

This is different with internal amplified dangers because we can't judge them as well. When it comes to personal and interpersonal concepts and experiences, they aren't as easy to predict or measure based on the variables. Meaning instead of attempting to analyse the threat before us, we start catastrophising and amplifying the danger to ourselves.

Sticking with the fear of inadequacy, this is something that has the potential to extend into every area of your life. Public speaking is often one of them. When you're about to make a public appearance or speech, whatever the occasion, you fear not being good enough to present

your speech well. You fear making a mistake. From this, you start imagining every single thing that could possibly go wrong. But what's often the case is that you give the speech with little to no hiccups, do a great job, are praised for it, and move on.

You amplified the danger in your head, made experiencing the pain of fear so much worse, and even risked being completely limited by the fear and not stepping forwards to do the speech at all. That is why this book is only focussed on amplified internal dangers that create your unconscious permanent internal fears.

If you'd like to experiment with the practices and exploration of your physical fears while going through this book, I encourage you to do so. But every type of fear and danger is not my focus. Instead, my desire is to dive deep into the real threat to you (your unconscious permanent internal fears), rather than the fears you can, and have been, processing on your own.

Therefore, if you're willing to accept that you have been amplifying your dangers and creating unconscious permanent internal fears with them that do not deserve the trust and respect you've been giving them, please join me in chapter two.

Let me summarise chapter one, as I know we've covered a lot here:

 There are multiple forms of fears, including physical, internal, temporary, and permanent.

Conscious fears are those you've knowingly chosen to adopt and keep for your growth and well-being.

Unconscious fears are those that you're hosting simply out of instinctive fear, without questioning whether they are worthy of your trust and respect.

Unconscious permanent internal fears are a danger to you. You should not blindly trust them.

The black cat represents your amplified dangers that don't pose as severe a threat to you in reality as you believe.

Call to Action: Have a think about your fears and see if you can start distinguishing them between the different types we've explored here. Do you know what your unconscious permanent internal fears are? Do you know which dangers you're amplifying?

Chapter Two

Safety in Fear

Unconscious permanent internal fears stay with you until you make a conscious and committed effort to let them go.

They thrive in the dark recess of your mind, but make no mistake—they are not hiding. In fact, they boldly leave clues for you to find, daring you to acknowledge their presence and confront them head-on.

To put it more aptly, unconscious permanent internal fears are like rats. They sneak into your mental home, and devour your precious thoughts and emotions. They gnaw away at your peace, leaving chaos in their wake. You used to coexist with these inner demons, believing you were powerless to evict them. Maybe you even lived with them for so long they seemed normal—an unchangeable part of your existence.

But now, you have taken decisive action against them. You bought this book, after all—which means you decided it's time to take control. It is time to clean house and get rid of these fear-ridden rodents you, unknowingly, chose to live with.

From here on out, we will call unconscious permanent internal fears what they truly are: the rats. It's time you deal with them once and for all.

Living Through Rats

Rather than imposing your will and presence onto them, you subconsciously chose to live around theirs. You adapted to coexist with them—adjusting to their demands.

Over time, with the rats living in your mind for so long, you lost the ability to differentiate between yourself and them. Instead, they became a part of you. You merged with them, becoming a human vessel carrying a mind filled with rats.

To live in harmony with the rats, you relinquished control and allowed them to take the lead. They were given top priority in your conscious thoughts, behaviours, and actions. You submitted to their dominance.

You see, this isn't a simple roommate situation, where two parties share a space but leave each other alone. No, the rats shape and guide every aspect of your life.

They do more than just occupy your mind. They monitor your every thought and action with a critical,

unrelenting eye. Every piece of information coming your way is filtered by them, twisted until you can't see the world for what it truly is.

You don't live with them; you live from them—not just *with* fear, but *from* fear.

What a painful way to live.

As long as the rats remain, they will torture you. And they won't leave until you make them leave.

Look around you for evidence. We all know someone— or perhaps, we *are* someone—who demands that everyone in their life tiptoes around their insecurities, no matter how irrational or unreasonable they may be. Like someone who has a deep insecurity in their looks and demands you spend a ridiculous amount of time taking photos of them before they're satisfied.

And when you don't play along, they lash out—not in anger, but in fear.

They panic because you challenged their decision to live through their rats. You didn't make it easier for them to live through their fears. By refusing to give their insecurities precedence and not agreeing to revolve your life around their fears (which you absolutely shouldn't do), you made it uncomfortable for that person to coexist with their rats.

How long can you deal with other people's fears for them, after all?

Comfortable Fear

The person who chose to endure the nasty rats did so with a subconscious acceptance. Somewhere along the way, they made the decision to coexist with these creatures—their unconscious permanent internal fears—and embrace their presence. They became convinced there was no way to rid themselves of the rats, so they made peace with them instead.

They decided to become hospitable to their fears.

It may seem strange to suggest that they could be comfortable living in fear, but I'm willing to bet they *have* become comfortable living a life wherein they spend every moment feeling afraid. I'll take it one step further, though: Not only have they chosen to accept the existence of the rats inside them, but they've also developed the habit of seeking comfort from them.

They turn to the rats to feel safe and at ease.

This sense of comfort is built upon a foundation of feeling safe—at least, safe enough. Think about your own life. There's something about the environment you're in, whether internal or external, that provides just enough security to make fear feel familiar—maybe even like home.

You feel safer when you feel afraid. You convinced yourself that staying in a state of fear is a less dangerous way of life than facing or fighting your fears. You built a life around the constant presence of fear, and you believe that as long as you keep your rats close, you won't get hurt.

In the depths of your mind, you've attached yourself to an identity of victimhood. The weight of your past and present pain has convinced you that you are powerless. Helpless. You believe there is nothing you can do.

The part of you that has grown accustomed to fear is now larger and stronger than the part that wants to be fearless.

Right now, in the battle between fearful comfort and growth, comfort is winning.

The Killer Comfort Blanket

Imagine fearful comfort as a warm, fluffy blanket. The softest material caresses your skin, wrapping you in its perfect weight—the kind of blanket you could lose yourself in for hours. It's a cocoon of safety and happiness, and you never want to leave its embrace.

But this seemingly innocent blanket is actually a dangerous criminal—a murderer, in fact. The infamous killer comfort blanket has been designed with one sinister purpose: to slowly kill its wearer's potential and growth without their knowledge. It's a skilled assassin disguised as a cozy throw. Billions were manufactured with one target—your willpower.

Who created them and why, you ask? The rats—your unconscious permanent internal fears—created the killer comfort blankets to stop you from wanting to evict them from your mental home. If the rats could manufacture

a weapon to manipulate their host into becoming comfortable in their painful presence, they'd never have to worry about being exterminated.

The killer comfort blanket slowly drains your willpower—your true potential and motivation. Your drive to do and be *anything else*. Before you know it, you're stuck within its deadly embrace, unwilling to break free. It kills your willpower, and in turn, it kills you.

The blanket kills you by whispering sweet lies, making you believe that wearing it means you are safe, that the rats will keep you safe. It convinces you that what you have right now, wrapped in the blanket with the rats ruling your mind, is all you'll ever need for peace and happiness.

You believe life without wearing this blanket—without suffering in constant fearful comfort—is not worth living.

Logistically speaking, there's not much you can do while wrapped up in a blanket. Your movements are limited to sitting, lying down, and perhaps a short walk. That's it. There's nothing else. If you won't risk an inch of your skin being exposed to the cold, you won't do *anything*. You systematically refuse to make yourself uncomfortable by removing the blanket—meaning you live in constant fearful comfort.

And so, you stop living.

You don't explore new places, try new things, or challenge yourself. You don't learn new skills. You don't do anything your rats convince you is unsafe.

But true life is about growth. It's about pushing past our comfort zones—something this dangerous blanket

will never allow you to experience. Because comfort kills growth—and vice versa.

By allowing yourself to become comfortable with something that causes you constant pain and suffering, you betrayed yourself. By surrendering your autonomy to your fears, you abandoned the reality you *deserve* to experience.

You betrayed yourself by refusing to acknowledge the truth: The rats (your unconscious permanent internal fears) and killer comfort blanket (the fearful comfort) are doing more harm than good. They are deceiving you. The very things you believe are protecting you are actually sabotaging you. Limiting you.

It's a toxic deception.

Time to wake up.

Fear vs. Fear

Believing you are safe in the presence of the rats and killer comfort blanket—two things that are real dangers to you—means one thing: You want to live with the fear more than you want to live without it.

You believe that by staying here, wrapped in fear, you are protected from the dangers lurking around you. That as long as you stay on guard, aware of every potential threat, you can avoid being harmed.

This may not sound like the reality of living through the rats and in the killer comfort blanket, i.e., remaining

on guard at all times, but it is. That's what fearful comfort is. You've become comfortable living in the constant pain of fear.

In this, you choose to continue the same subconscious responses you've always relied on. You don't want to stop being scared, so you're not going to do anything to change that. You don't want to change your situation, so you're not going to start doing anything differently. You don't want to.

What's the difference between convincing yourself that you do not want to live in fear anymore and actually committing to change? How do you even make that transition?

Well, the first indicator is a willingness to make yourself temporarily uncomfortable for the sake of your growth. Then it's about taking steps to enact that. When it comes to your fears, being temporarily uncomfortable means facing your fears—instead of blindly trusting them and avoiding doing anything to question and remove them.

Let me share one piece of advice on how you can make the transition from fearful comfort to fear-facing growth. Have a read and try it out. It might sound contradictory and confusing to you, that I suggest you fight fear with fear, but not all fears are harmful. Some are incredibly helpful. The distinction being that the helpful ones are consciously created by you to fear anything that is harming what you value most. For me, that is my peace, happiness, and growth.

Therefore what I suggest is that you create a bigger conscious permanent internal fear. You deliberately choose

to be afraid of something more than your current fear, and use that fear to drive your decisions and actions against your rats.

As an example, I have created a conscious permanent internal fear of my rats—my unconscious permanent internal fears. I am afraid of how they manipulate, sabotage, and limit me. I take the threat they pose to me incredibly seriously. I don't want to live the rest of my life blindly trusting fears that are, frankly, untrustworthy. They don't deserve me living my life based on what they tell me will keep me safe when I haven't even had the chance to decide whether something is a danger to me or not.

The things driving my journey to face and fight my rats are my fear of them as well as my anger at them (explored in chapter twelve). My fear is of the harm they have caused and can continue to cause. My internal survival relies on my willingness and commitment to eliminate my unconscious permanent internal fears. That's why I call them rats.

This brings us to the end of part one of the book, covering the theory of fears. Next we will explore what it means to face our fears in part two. Before we move on, a summary of chapter two:

 The rats represent your unconscious permanent internal fears.

 You're not only living with your fears; you're living through them.

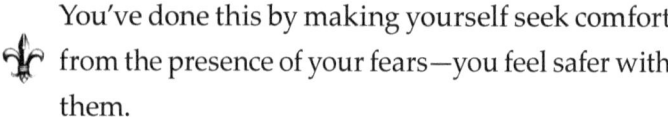 You've done this by making yourself seek comfort from the presence of your fears—you feel safer with them.

 The killer comfort blanket represents your fearful comfort situation.

You can change your decision to stay in fearful comfort.

One way to do this is by creating a conscious permanent internal fear that is bigger than your rats.

Call to Action: Try to identify where in your life you are staying in fearful comfort, wrapped in the killer comfort blanket.

PART TWO

Facing Fears

Chapter Three

Facing

When you refuse to change your fearful comfort environment, you are instead choosing to keep repeating the same reactions that served you before. You don't want to change your situation, so why bother trying something new? And because you don't want to stop being afraid, you don't take any actions to overcome that fear.

So what are you choosing to do instead?

Sometimes you freeze—paralysed by panic, unable to think clearly, unable to act (chapter five). Other times, you run—fleeing as fast as you can, trying to escape something that feels impossible to outrun (chapter six). Your response depends on more factors than you may realise. These will be explored throughout parts three and four of the book.

As there are multiple rats hiding in your mind, each one represents a different fear, with its own black cat (amplified danger). You've been responding to each one in its own unique way. You've also been responding to the *same rat* in multiple ways. You'll freeze from a fear one day and run away the next.

To change those responses consciously, you'll need to thoroughly face each fear, how you've been reacting to them, and why you've been doing that. This journey is split into parts two, three, and four of the book. Each part is essential, as you need to face every aspect of your fear in order to understand it.

Why is this? Well, you've been acting out subconscious responses to your rats mostly because of a lack of information about what you're doing and why you're doing it, as well as a refusal to thoroughly investigate the validity of the threat severity you believe the black cats are posing to you.

You've been avoiding looking closer at your fears, instead looking away—afraid because it feels easier, safer, or you believe it's the only thing you can do. I want you to do the exact opposite, which is what this book will guide you through. Then, once you've gained all the information you need, you'll either have enough evidence to disprove your beliefs in the fear entirely, or you'll be equipped to understand what you need to do to fight your fear. Fighting fears is explored in volume two of the Fear Series, because you can't fight what you don't know.

And right now, when it comes to your rats and yourself, there is a lot you don't know. One could even say that you have an abundance of mental blind spots: Hidden corners of your mind that stay in the dark because you're too afraid to shine a light on them. Afraid of what you may find.

BS Boxes

Imagine your blind spots as solid, unmovable black boxes. We'll call them "bs boxes" for short. Each one is about the size of a football, and they show up right at your feet whenever you're in a situation where those blind spots come into play.

You see, blind spots take the form of truths within yourself that you haven't seen and are refusing to see. This is usually from a fear or identity belief system—everything you believe about your fears and identity stops you from learning information that can change those beliefs into something different.

As you move through life, these bs boxes keep appearing, blocking your path. You know they're there. You see them and feel them. But the idea of opening them and finding out what's inside? It's too much. So, instead, you avoid them. You look away, act like they don't exist, and carry on.

The problem is that ignoring them doesn't make them go away. Running and freezing doesn't do anything, as your bs boxes follow you everywhere, a constant reminder

of your unresolved fears and every part of you left in the dark. They only vanish once they've been opened.

It's funny, though, as what often happens is that when you finally see them, they feel like the most obvious things in the world. They were right in front of you the whole time, you just refused to accept it.

Allow me to demonstrate. In my fear of inadequacy, the main area of my life this came into play was my studies. I was a dedicated perfectionist, and anything less than the highest grade felt like a failure to me. And in this fear, I dedicated every minute of my life to not make my fear come true—failing my exams. I suffered in my fear but also sacrificed a lot of joy and experienced growth. And yes, everyone needs to study. No one should do it out of permanent fear, though.

Anyway, my blind spot was the fact that every time I got the highest grade, I didn't feel anything. I felt a second of satisfaction that I hadn't failed, and that was it. Move on to the next one. No celebration. No increased confidence. Not once did my hard work ever convince me that I wasn't inadequate.

I had so much evidence before me to disprove my fear and beliefs, but I wasn't ready to see and accept any of it. I knew I was miserable and was only working so hard out of personal fear, afraid of what it might say about me. But I didn't stop to open the bs box before me after every exam to realise that I wasn't getting what I wanted.

Every time I had an exam, I'd think, *This is the one that's going to make me feel better.* But it never did. I was tripping

on bs boxes all over the place. It took me years to realise that my efforts weren't giving me the results I longed for.

I was working so hard to avoid making my fear into a reality without getting what I really craved—not living in the fear of inadequacy anymore. Then, when I finally opened this box and saw this truth, I pivoted my focus and efforts to figuring out what would allow me to earn what I wanted the most. What would change my experience of life the most.

The Residence

Imagine your internal self living in a complex and intricate home—a mental residence where every part of you exists. This is your sanctuary of thoughts and emotions, your personal space.

But right now this home is, frankly, a mess. The lights are either broken or switched off, there is clutter everywhere, and heavy curtains are blocking the windows, keeping you from seeing the outside world. The air is stale and musty, thick from a lack of fresh air. There's a stench you can't place but don't want to imagine the source of.

And that's only within the single room you've been living in. You see, you're not the only one who's been living here. The rats and black cats have also called it home for many years. Not only that, they've taken over.

Many years ago, the rats lulled you into a small room with a killer comfort blanket, and you haven't left since.

Your awareness of the black cats lurking, trust in the rats to keep you safe, and delusioned comfort of living wrapped within the blanket stole all of your willpower to leave.

This means you don't know of the current chaos that exists from the rats and black cats reigning over your inner home.

But this is *your* home. It's meant to be your sanctuary, a place where you are at peace. Only you have the power to decide its condition and who gets to stay within it. Ideally, it should be only you—along with any loving presences you choose to invite in. You deserve a home that's clean, filled with light and fresh air, a place that wraps you in real safety.

And because it's your home, you are the only one with the power to transform it. Only you can tidy up the mess and evict the rats and black cats. Only you can open all the bs boxes that have cluttered it, throw open the windows, and let the sunlight and fresh air pour in.

Then, you can renovate and redecorate it, turning your mental home into the most beautiful sanctuary you can imagine. Whether it's a cosy lakeside retreat or a beachside haven, it can be whatever you dream it to be.

And now that you know your residence can be anything you want it to be, that you don't have to let the rats and black cats reign in chaos, that's exactly what you're going to do.

How? This first process—cleaning your mental residence by opening the bs boxes and turning on all the lights—is exactly what you'll do by facing your fears. You'll

learn the information previously hidden in the dark by asking internal questions for each fear.

While you've been blindly living in one room of your internal residence, you've lost awareness of the exact layout of your home, meaning you don't know what the function of every room is and what is held inside. Therefore, picture each fear as occupying its own room in this house. Each room—each fear—houses its own black cat, rats, and bs boxes.

For each fear, you'll need to open the door and face what's inside. First, you'll analyse the rats—your fears themselves. You'll probe into understanding what they've been making you do. This will be explored in chapters three, five (freezing), and six (running).

Then you'll look closer at the black cats—the amplified dangers. You'll learn what you believe about them, and what makes them such a threat to you. This will be explored in chapters three and four, and all of part four.

While you're facing the rats and black cats, you'll also be opening the bs boxes scattered around the room. You don't know what you'll find and when, though it will be enlightening. This is explored throughout all of parts two, three, and four.

As you see everything, the bs boxes will vanish once opened, and you'll lose your trust in the rats, and thus your fear of the black cats, and evict them both. Whether they dissipate as soon as you stop believing in them or you have to take more conscious actions later (fighting stage in volume two), you'll make them leave.

And so, finally, you will no longer have to live through rats, afraid of black cats. You'll burn the killer comfort blankets and be a pro at opening bs boxes.

In the end, you'll make your internal home into a space that reflects what you truly want it to be. It will be a sanctuary of peace. You will not let anyone else dictate what your home looks like or how it feels anymore. This is your space, and for the first time, you're about to fully claim it.

Funnelling

How do you face your deepest fears? How do you open the door and then open all of your bs boxes to see your hidden truths? All of your emotional clutter, doubts, and anxieties? There isn't exactly a physical room you can walk into or a box you can open, so how is it actually done?

The method I propose is called the "funnelling approach." While this technique is often used in fields like advocacy, we're going to tailor it for your personal journey.

If you're unfamiliar with it, the general idea is that you start your investigation with a broad theme or question, looking at the overarching topic tied to your fears. Then, little by little, you narrow your focus, digging deeper into specific areas as you uncover more insights. Think of it as peeling back the layers of an onion—starting with the outer layer and working your way inwards until you get to the core. Once you can see the web entirely, you can finally

start to untangle it. By using the funnelling approach, you'll systematically work through your fears, their strands and elements, uncovering how they impact each other and you as a whole.

Why do I suggest this approach? Well, it's better than having no plan at all. Plus, it's more effective than randomly tackling isolated fears and their elements without understanding how they connect. You need to see the whole picture because your fears don't exist in solitude—they're part of a complex web. Every strand represents a form of your fear, and all of them are interconnected, influencing and reinforcing one another.

I have organised the facing journey into parts two, three, and four of the book. Part two covers choosing a fear, then diving into its danger and pulling strands. Part three covers facing your response to that fear so far, and part four explores three topics that may be influencing why you're responding the way you are.

I encourage you to read these chapters sequentially, and do the suggested actions in each one in that order. I urge you to not skip any steps just because they make you uncomfortable or scared. That discomfort—that fear—is the very heart of this journey. Yes, you're going to be uncomfortable. Yes, you'll find truths about yourself that may be hard to accept. But this is an essential part of the journey. It's kind of the whole point.

Try the whole process once, then take some time to reflect on your experience. Did it help? Did you learn anything about your fears and yourself? Did it feel

overwhelming? Were there parts that didn't work for you? Whatever your experience, pick and choose the parts you want to do again and create a new process for yourself based on what you need for the next time you select a fear to face.

Once you've worked through this process, you'll find yourself empowered—specifically, you'll have earned the power of knowledge. In my experience, simply learning enough information to disprove my beliefs around my fears allowed me to easily change those beliefs and no longer fear that experience. I realised I was wasting my time and energy fearing something that didn't really pose much danger to me at all, which then means that with these new beliefs, whenever I experience it in the future, the pain really is minimal. And even if that's not the case, and it is an uncomfortable situation, I don't start fearing it again. Instead, I choose to heal and learn from the experience to grow—not stay stagnant in my painful state of perpetual fear.

Whereas, for other fears, more is necessary, which is where the fighting stage comes in (we'll get to that in volume two). What do I mean by this? Well, sometimes the power of knowledge isn't the only power you need to earn. You need more, like the power of honesty or healing. Sometimes you need to do or experience the exact thing you're afraid of to realise there was nothing to fear.

Either way, facing your fears changes *everything*. Avoiding it doesn't.

To help you see everything clearly, I encourage you to create an ongoing physical mind map throughout this internal exploration. Digital or pen and paper. Whatever you prefer. I love the Concepts app on my iPad, as it has endless canvas. I pay to use the feature where I can move things I've written. My whole book was written using this, and I also use it for journaling.

Use this mind map to record everything you learn and realise, every connection you uncover. Figure out which areas are lacking in clarity, and go deeper. Ask more questions to see more.

This journey will challenge you—it might even feel overwhelming at times—but I believe in you. You are more than capable of finding your true self and stepping into your power. This is your chance to face your fears and take control of your life. You've got this.

Pick a Fear

Pick your biggest, strongest fear. The one that feels like it's always there, influencing everything you do.

I want you to start here because your biggest growth comes from facing the fears that have the strongest hold on you. Letting go of even one deep internal fear can have an exponential impact on your life. This might sound like a bold claim, but think about it: One fear—one rat—ripples through so many areas of your life, shaping your choices and behaviours in ways you don't realise.

When you carry these fears, they're always in the background, simmering away, and your mind is constantly working to avoid the black cats, i.e., the amplified dangers.

By facing your deepest fear, you're not just breaking free from it—you're uncovering a version of yourself that's been hidden away. This journey is so much more than fear; it's about removing one layer of your scared self at a time to slowly uncover the true you.

Your first step on this journey should be to tackle your greatest fear, because once you have, every other one will seem smaller in comparison. Plus, your new experience of living without that form of anxiety will motivate you to keep moving forwards.

But how do you figure out which fear is your greatest? How do you choose? For some people, this is an easy decision—you already know your biggest fear because it's all you ever think about. If this is you, then great. You're ready to move on to the next step.

If it isn't so obvious for you to figure out which fear has the strongest hold on your life, start by asking yourself: Which fear do I feel the most? What am I most anxious about? Out of everything, what am I most afraid of happening? Remember, we're only focussing on internal fears here, though.

Take some time to reflect on your thoughts, feelings, and actions. Note them down in your mind map. As you do, you'll hopefully find it. But if you're still unsure, that's okay too. You can start with any fear you feel ready to face. You just need to start.

Identify the General Danger

Now that you've chosen your fear, it's time to dig deeper and understand exactly what terrifies you. This might feel scary—no one likes to face their darkest fears, after all. But that's exactly what you're going to do. You will break down this rat, understand it from every angle, and pinpoint the danger it represents.

At its core, fear is your survival instinct. It activates when your mind identifies a threat it believes could harm you. To free yourself from this rat, you need to clearly understand the nature of the threat it represents.

When you first named your fear, you likely thought of it as a single isolated issue. Take, for example, the fear of losing a specific loved one. This fear lingers in your mind, stealing your peace because the idea of life without that person feels unbearable. It's not just about their absence— it's the pain, the emptiness, and the grief that you dread.

This fear is very common, but it's more than just about being afraid of that person passing away. It's the fear of loss in general. There are also the fears of grief and loneliness connected with it. This is how you start being able to map out your web of fears and how they connect. Every specific situational fear you have is connected to one or multiple broader general dangers.

To truly understand your fear, you need to step back and look at the bigger picture. What are the general dangers that make this situational one seem

so powerful? List them all out. Then you can move on to the next step in the fear-facing journey in chapter four, which is to pull the strands apart.

To conclude chapter three, let's summarise:

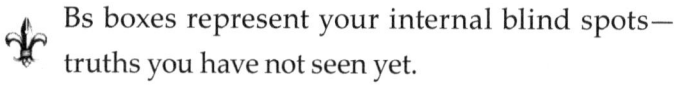 Bs boxes represent your internal blind spots— truths you have not seen yet.

The residence represents your internal home.

Create an ongoing mind map of your fear-facing journey, noting down all of your discoveries.

I suggest a funnelling approach when facing your fears.

Start the journey of facing your fears by picking your greatest fear.

Then identify the general danger that situational fear is related to.

Call to Action: Try to identify your greatest internal fear. Which one haunts you the most? And what is the general danger, or multiple dangers, associated with it?

Chapter Four

Pulling Strands

Now you can begin the process of pulling strands. A strand is a single specific situational fear, linked to the general fear you've identified. Your fear of loss, for instance, will manifest in many forms, such as loss of people, money, safety, or opportunity. And every one of these strands must be pulled away from the tangled web of your general danger to truly see it all and address the root.

This is essential because if even one strand of your general danger remains, the fear itself stays alive. You might feel less afraid than before, but it'll still linger, ready to assert itself.

As you're going through life, the strands will become mental loopholes to your efforts to be fearless. You'll ask, "But what if this happens?" believing you don't have

enough evidence to disprove your fear altogether. If you try to tackle the general fear head-on without addressing the strands, they'll sneak up behind you and yank you back in.

Imagine it like pulling apart a stick of string cheese, one strand at a time. Separate your general fear into strands of specific situational fears so you can face every form.

You do this by listing out all the ways you're afraid of being harmed by the general fear. Write down everything you are afraid could go wrong.

Fear of Change

Let's dive into the fear of change as an example.

This fear is fascinating, because it has the dual nature of being both powerful and disempowering. It's powerful in that the scope of limitation and damage it can inflict upon its victim is endless. At the same time, it's disempowering because it makes people fear the one thing that will empower them the most: an ownership of change.

Widely held, the fear of change can be overwhelming—there are so many versions of it because change is multidimensional. It's also a permanent part of our lives. Everything is temporary because everything can and will change—it is impossible to avoid or outrun.

Change may well be the only permanent part of life after all, other than death.

Why do you fear it, then? What is it about change that makes you believe it to be a threat? And are you aware

that this fear limits your ability to smoothly navigate and handle all transitions and changes in your life?

Being afraid of change means you have a negative belief system about it. You believe that change is a bad thing. More than that, you believe it's dangerous and harmful.

By labelling change as a threat, you avoid it. In this choice of fearful stagnation, the only growth you're experiencing is the form that's essentially been forced upon you by the Universe. Your refusal to easily glide through transformation has limited you to those that are quite painful to experience.

Yes, there are changes that are inherently painful, but it's because they challenge the deepest parts of you that you stubbornly don't want to let go of. These forms of growth are often imposed upon you because you're either unwilling or unable to start them yourself. This form of transformation is a universal experience.

However, it's not the only kind of change available to you. When you start seeing change as a good thing and take ownership of it, it becomes quite easy—practically enjoyable—because you recognise it as an upgrade. Seeing change as an opportunity rather than a threat allows you to actively claim it as your own and use it to transform yourself, your life, and your relationships into what truly fulfills you. You can take pride in becoming the person you consciously decided to be by choosing to change.

Let me now show you what pulling strands looks like. The first three are common fears you may be facing—and the fourth is the one I believe to be the greatest of all.

Strand One - Fear of Changing Yourself

In itself, this strand has many strands of its own. Many do. You realise that when asking yourself the questions: How exactly do you fear changing yourself? Who is it you are afraid to become?

Maybe you're afraid of becoming someone new and different. But different in what way? Different from the people you're close to? Different from what everyone expects you to be? Different from the person you thought you wanted to be?

Who you want to be will keep changing. You should and will grow in unexpected ways, but this can be hard to accept because you lose your understanding of yourself. This happens because you only know the one version of who you've always been. You've become comfortable with being that version and don't want to become uncomfortable. At the same time, those around you also likely find comfort in knowing and understanding a specific version of you.

To move past this fear, try seeing it in a new light. Changing into someone new and different is truly exciting. It's alchemy and transformation.

What it isn't, is a danger to you.

Can you challenge yourself to believe that?

Strand Two - Fear of Not Being Able to Change Yourself

This fear is common among people who tried to change some part of themselves in the past without success. Quitting addiction is a prime example.

When pulling strands apart, you might realise that your first failed attempt at self-change led to the belief that you can't change.

Failing at the beginning of a challenge often eliminates the little confidence you started with—especially if you haven't consciously developed a solid mindset to prevent that from happening.

When you try to change and fail again, it unfortunately reinforces your belief that change is impossible. You feel worse, lose hope, and now have more evidence to support the idea that you can't change.

Sadly, you haven't been building or nurturing any positive beliefs to counteract these negative ones, allowing them to grow stronger. This results in a kind of self-fulfilling prophecy.

However, no reality exists where you can't change yourself. You can. Can it be difficult? Absolutely. No one said it wouldn't be a challenge. That doesn't mean it isn't possible, only that you need to put more effort and effective strategy into your endeavour.

What's one thing that you can do today to change yourself in the ways you desire? What strategies have you

used in the past? I have three strategies I use to make sure I change myself in the ways I need to, especially when I'm finding it difficult. The first is aimed at starting a new habit, and the second two are aimed at stopping a habit or behaviour I don't want to continue doing.

The first strategy I use to start a new habit is I ease myself into it. I've found that I'm not very good at sticking to new regimens when I rush into them, get overwhelmed, and struggle to integrate them into my life. I used to start things, like exercise, based on the regimen and consistency other people told me I should be doing, so if I struggled to keep up with that, I'd lose confidence and be fighting with more than a simple change in habits. Instead, I changed my strategy and now start things in a way that is sustainable for me. Then as I progress, I increase the intensity at the right time.

The second is going cold turkey off the habit. It may sound like repeated advice, but it really is the only thing that I've been successful with. Trying to wean off something doesn't work for me. I have to completely stop and not allow myself to even think about it. Bringing in something new and exciting to take my attention can help sometimes as well.

The third strategy is I identify my triggers and cut myself off from them. Say you want to stop being on social media as much. I would delete the apps. Get rid of them, and start living without them. And if I love my new reality, then I delete my accounts. By eliminating your access to it, you make yourself find something else to do.

These are some strategies I use to change myself, and they work for me. I've tried different things to see what I do and don't respond to. Test different strategies and discover what works for you. This is all part of finding yourself and then changing yourself into who you really want to be. It can feel overwhelming if you try to do everything at once, but all you need to do is start with one.

Strand Three - Fear of Someone Not Changing into the Person You Want to Change Them into

This fear is a very specific example I've used to demonstrate the point of pulling strands and how specific to your situation they can be. Yes, there are many ways someone can be afraid of their loved one not changing.

This strand focuses on the specific fear created when you enter into a relationship with someone because you see them as a project to improve. Whether it's a romantic or platonic relationship, you connect with them because you want to, in some way, "fix" them.

In that intention and endeavour, you established an unhealthy, and even damaging, relationship dynamic. Plus, you created a fear that is both unnecessary and unhelpful, as it stops you from seeing the true nature of the situation.

You fear someone not changing because you want to change them. For this strand, we're focussing on this desire

for someone to be a specific way, likely emerging early in your relationship.

Fixing a Fixer-Upper

If you hold the fear that someone you love won't change, then you may have started the relationship with them because you saw them as a fixer-upper. In your own way, with your own reasons, you began a relationship with someone because you wanted to improve them, believing you had the ability and right to do so.

You intended to invest yourself into transforming this person into exactly what you want them to be. Your intention in the relationship isn't about mutual growth and development. You don't want them to see and treat you as a fixer-upper or to grow together. No, you solely want to have your hand in shaping, fixing, or saving them.

What you want that person to be depends on your personal wants and needs, such as wanting a boyfriend who always does PDA with you, and yet it makes him incredibly uncomfortable. The common ground for seeing someone as a fixer-upper is wanting to change them in ways to specifically meet your wants and needs. Their development is really aimed at satisfying you, not them or your relationship itself.

You might *believe* you want them to change for your mutual benefit or, more nobly, for their own benefit. But, to truly understand if your fear of them not changing stems

from an unhealthy relationship dynamic, you need to examine the changes you want them to make.

Are your reasons for wanting these changes solely for your benefit?

Changes for mutual relationship development are excellent. They're also consensual, as they happen with agreement from both parties, who are willing to change in certain ways for their own benefit and that of the relationship. There are no hidden intentions. No breaching of consent.

On the other hand, if you want someone to change solely to meet your own desires and needs, without clearly communicating this and without being prepared to reciprocate, you are being deceitful, hypocritical, and unfairly demanding. This may sound harsh, but you must question whether it really is your truth.

Have you found yourself complaining about and fearing someone not changing into something specific just because it would benefit you? Are they aware of that? Have they genuinely agreed to being treated that way in the relationship? Would they benefit from making those changes even if they weren't in a relationship with you? Have you and are you willing to make similar changes for them?

These are crucial questions you need to consider when dealing with this strand of the fear of change. The other person likely didn't enter the relationship because they wanted to be your fixer-upper. They probably aren't in it simply because they want you to change them. They could

hire a coach or mentor for that. The question you need to repeatedly ask yourself regarding this fear is whether that person genuinely wants to change in the way you want them to.

If they don't, then there's no point in fearing them not changing. They won't change if they don't want to. You can't force them and shouldn't try to.

If they do want to transform into who you want them to be, then it's important to question their motives. Why do they want to change in the way you're directing them? Do they truly agree with you? Do they believe you and agree with you when you say these changes are best for them and your relationship?

Or are they simply trying to impress you? Are they willing to do anything in their need for your love, approval, and attention? Are they willing to lose themselves, their identity, their self-respect, and their freedom in that quest?

And is that really someone you want to be in a relationship with?

Did you pick someone insecure as a fixer-upper because you knew they were vulnerable, and you wanted to use it for your personal benefit? Does their vulnerability provide you with something you secretly crave? Does it offer you attention and a sense of control? Is it revealing a darker side of you that requires light and healing?

In this process of facing your fears, you are questioning them. And by questioning your fears, you're actually questioning yourself.

Is this fear truly justified? Have you considered the reasons, causes, and motivations behind it? Did you reach the conclusion that it's essential to your well-being? Or, when you pulled the strand apart and dissected it, did you realise it's not reasonable enough to justify the constant pain of living in fear?

Do you honestly want to keep being afraid that your loved ones won't change? Or are you going to examine the fear and use your rational thinking to see it's not a wise fear to keep?

On asking and answering these questions for yourself, you may wonder, *What now?* I have this information, and I don't know what to do with it. Well, what do you want to do with it? Maybe you want to stay the way you are and are happy to be that way. Maybe you do want to change things but don't know how or are afraid.

Which brings us back to strands one and two, and the fears of changing yourself and not being able to change yourself. This is a prime example of how the strands of a general danger can be interconnected and affect each other. This is why the rats—unconscious permanent internal fears—are so dangerous. You're not only dealing with one sabotaging and limiting fear. You're dealing with many, which are affecting and amplifying each other as well.

That's why the facing journey and pulling strands can be so helpful. Identifying exactly what all the forms of your fear are shows you what factors are affecting your decision-making so far. Now that you're aware of them, you can watch out for how they are attempting to affect

your current decisions and can consciously ignore their input into your decision-making process. You can stop living and making decisions out of fear.

That's the point of this work. You find afraid parts and versions of yourself, and you get rid of them. So you can give yourself the chance to live as the true you.

Strand Four - Fear of Bad Change

So far, we've explored a few strands of the fear of change to demonstrate how a single overarching general fear can manifest in multiple specific forms, and I've saved the biggest for last: the fear of bad change. This is one of the most common fears worldwide.

The fear of bad change has many substrands of its own. Take a minute to think about all the aspects of your life where you are afraid of a negative change—relationships, community, recreations, careers. The possibilities are literally endless.

It's humbling to realise you don't have the power to stop these changes from happening. Ultimately, anything can happen, and you can't stop most of it, which can be terrifying.

Fear of bad health, financial changes, safety, and family dynamics—it can be overwhelming, but it's important to keep pushing forwards and continue facing them, one by one. You will keep feeling the pain of their existence until

you extinguish them. Facing them fully is the first phase of that.

Substrand - Fear of Bad Health Changes

I used to be afraid of becoming helplessly ill.

This fear was triggered when I witnessed my grandmother, Mama Ji (pronounced Mam-a Jee), Surinder Kaur Randhawa, suffer from a disease similar to Parkinson's. I was around thirteen years old, and my bedroom was right above hers, which was next to the bathroom. For almost a year, when she woke in the middle of the night to use the bathroom, she often fell on her way there. She was about sixty-two years old. Each night, I heard her fall and rushed downstairs to help her.

That's where it all began. Every day, it broke my heart to see her trapped helplessly in her own body. In her final months, Mama Ji was essentially paralysed, reduced to skin and bones. My grandmother suffered a lot during the last five years of her life before she passed away in July 2018 at the age of sixty-seven.

This experience changed me—and my family—forever. It matured me. Taught me empathy and respect for my elders and those battling health issues. But it also made me very afraid. Seeing how much she suffered made me terrified of going through it myself or watching others I love suffer.

I carried this grief and fear for years. I was angry, believing it was wrong for Mama Ji to suffer in this way. Over time, though, I allowed myself to process and heal my pain. And in healing, I realised the gift we were blessed with. You see, my grandmother was a very independent woman. My grandfather, Papa Ji (pronounced Pap-a Jee), Gurdawar Singh Randhawa, passed away at forty-nine years old, so Mama Ji was a widow for nearly twenty years. When I was growing up, she wasn't soft or chatty or one who talked about feelings. She led a simple life, asking for little and expecting nothing from others. As a result, despite living with her all my life, I didn't know her very well.

That changed when she fell ill. Then she had no choice but to soften. She had to accept help. It was in this time that we truly got to know each other. It took Mama Ji becoming vulnerable, and me maturing, for us to form a genuine bond. I cared for her, and she let me. I loved making her laugh, and would sing to her at night. Ask her questions about life. I gave her my love and time in exchange for hers.

The relationship we built, what we shared together, shaped me forever. It grounded me in kindness and vulnerability. It gave me love and memories I will never lose. I received something special. And the truth is that without Mama Ji being ill, we wouldn't have grown closer the way we did. I wouldn't have developed the way I did.

In that journey, I developed in my spirituality and chose to change the beliefs and principles I live by to empower me, instead of feeding my victim mentality. It was too painful to experience life believing that goodness was not present in every situation. I had to challenge that belief and change it to be something that supports and inspires me instead.

Thus, I changed it to believing that every situation in our lives holds a lesson and/or blessing, instead of believing that events and experiences are either good or bad. My evidence showed me that they are often both. Where there is pain, there will be pleasure, and vice versa. It may be that the pain was the only way to experience that pleasure. Or maybe you need to wait a few months or years before you can find the pleasure. It will be there, though, as nature and the Universe exist in balance. You just have to look for the good.

I believe there's always a reason behind how the Universe shapes our lives. It's also always for our benefit—whether that benefit is teaching us a lesson we need to learn that is essential for our growth or it's a blessing or gift we need to receive. Embracing this belief allows me to see my life experiences in a more positive and empowering light. It helps me shift my perspective and appreciate the bigger picture.

You also have the ability to decide which principles and beliefs you live by, and whether they empower you or not (explored further in chapter eleven). The beliefs and principles guiding you can either help you or hinder you. You choose.

To conclude chapter four, and the end of part two, facing your fears is essential because it empowers you with

the knowledge you need to move forwards, away from living through your rats. Without this, you're navigating blind with bs boxes in your way. After going through the process in part two, you can either pick one strand you have identified in this journey to explore the topics in parts three and four of the book or you can read them as general topics and apply them to one of your fears later.

To summarise chapter four:

 The process for facing your fears begins by picking your biggest internal fear.

 Next, identify the general danger or dangers related to this.

 Then, break the general danger down into all of its strands, i.e., all of the specific situational fears you hold.

 Strands can then be pulled apart into substrands.

Call to Action: Using your greatest fear identified from the previous chapter, try to start pulling its strands apart. Drawing a mind map can be incredibly helpful for this.

PART THREE

Facing
the How

Chapter Five

Freezing

After you have begun the facing process from part two, I suggest that you choose one of the strands—specific situational fears—you've identified, and thoroughly explore all the topics covered in parts three and four of the book. In facing your fear, you need to see as many areas of it as possible. This is rooted in the following two topics: how you've been responding to the fear—understanding your behaviour and way of living and realising you can do something different instead; and why you've been responding the way you have, which is rooted in what you believe about the fear and danger.

I won't pretend to cover every topic you could possibly need to explore in facing your fears, as your fears are unique to you and your experiences. These are the foundation of

where you begin, though, as they cover topics that will likely affect every fear in some way.

Let's begin the journey of exploring how you've been responding to your fears by exploring the freeze response. Everyone knows what freezing before a physical threat looks like, as it is usually a physical freezing response. This is different with internal fears, as it can be harder to spot. The same goes with running, which is why I've dedicated a chapter to each response.

When a rat is present in your mind, it alerts you to the potential presence of its associated black cat—the amplified danger. And in the face of that potential danger, your mind often freezes. But how does your mind freeze when it sees danger?

The freeze response is an immobilising reaction, meaning it stops you in your tracks, focussing solely on the perceived threat. This primal, instinctual reaction causes both your mind and body to become rigid and unresponsive. It's like being trapped in a block of ice, unable to move or think clearly.

A physical freeze response looks like being stuck in a certain physical position, with your mind either blank, catastrophising the danger, or trying to make your body take action but struggling to do that.

An internal freeze looks like your mind focussing only on the threat, while also either going blank, catastrophising the danger, or knowing but not being able to take action. Usually, however, the only thing your mind does in a

freeze response is amplify the fear by imagining all the possible ways you could be harmed.

It puts all other thoughts on hold. Time slows down. Your surroundings blur and fade into the background as your mind halts all rational thought processes. Pure panic takes over.

You are left completely paralysed in the face of danger. By immobilising your mind, the freeze response strips you of your ability to assess the situation and consider your options.

You are defenseless.

Vulnerable to future attacks.

Frozen Willpower

The freeze response doesn't just paralyse your body and thoughts—it immobilises your willpower. It strips away not only your ability to reason but also your desire to respond. Your will is frozen, leaving you incapable of doing anything other than staying exactly where you are.

This defense mechanism has served you well in the past. The black cat has walked past you before without causing harm. And so, you stick to what's worked. Or maybe it was an instinctive reaction; you were simply too afraid to do anything else.

Either way, by choosing to freeze, you relinquish all control over yourself.

Your birthright—the power to guide your own mind, body, and will—now lies in the hands of the rats living within you. You handed them the reins. And now, they manipulate your actions at their whim.

Fear of Being Alone

The fear of being alone is an excellent example of an internal fear that most people respond to with a freeze response. To be clear, I am referring to staying in an unhealthy relationship out of the fear of being alone.

It's best understood by first relating to the black cat. The danger is a belief you hold. You believe that losing someone in your life will bring you pain, whether it's just one person or an entire group. You believe losing them is a danger to you, as you'll be in pain without them.

What kind of pain do you think you'd be in without them? It varies for each individual and situation. Some may feel their self-worth is tied to romantic relationships, believing that without a partner, they hold little value. They think not being in a relationship is a reflection of their own worthlessness. To avoid the pain of feeling worthless, they may stay in a bad relationship.

This fear, though commonly associated with romantic relationships, can manifest in any type of connection. It could be in your family, friendships, work relationships, or even social media. The source of the fear is irrelevant. What matters is the belief that your worth is directly linked to

you having a strong or public relationship with this person. Being connected to this person adds value to you and your experience of life, meaning you also believe that not being in a relationship with them reduces it.

In wanting to avoid encountering this danger, you freeze. In this state of panic, you are unable to assess the health or potential success of the relationship. Your fear clouds your judgment, preventing you from determining whether this person is truly good for you.

You are too afraid of them leaving to make a rational decision about their impact on your life.

This fear keeps you frozen in the relationship, unable to leave—even if you wanted to. The value of peace and well-being takes a back seat to comfort in this inner struggle.

Trapped in your fear, you become trapped in an unhealthy relationship. In choosing to stay frozen, you subject yourself to continued suffering. You willingly choose to endure fear and remain in the company of someone who does not contribute positively to your life.

Instead, you make excuses.

You turn a blind eye, avoiding the red flags. You don't address the issues you know need resolution. You convince yourself that things will get better. Or that you're overreacting. You choose to fear a worse pain, rather than believing the possibility of something better.

So, why do you stay frozen in these damaging relationships? The reasons will vary, but at the core lies a belief of powerlessness.

The Belief of Powerlessness

When you lack the belief that you are powerful, you fall into the trap of feeling powerless. Powerlessness becomes your truth, convincing you that you have nothing and you are nothing.

The belief (explored in chapter eight) in being powerful or powerless often depends on the situation. You'll feel powerful in one context and powerless in another. Power (explored in chapter nine) isn't uniform—it takes on different forms depending on how it's used. That's why it's essential to develop strong beliefs in all the forms of power you want to earn and access.

When it comes to fear, your belief in your own power shapes your entire response. If you believe your only option is to run, you'll run. If you believe you have the power to face it, you will. If you believe you can fight the rats and black cats, you'll do that too.

But if you believe you have no power at all, you'll freeze. And you keep freezing because you don't believe you can change that belief.

But neither of those beliefs are true.

You do have power. Unlimited internal power. You just need to activate it, claim it, and use it. Let yourself benefit from it.

You can also absolutely change your beliefs—and quickly too. There are different techniques you can try, and I will guide you through my favourite ones focussing

on powerlessness. Try them and see what works for you. The biggest advice I can give regarding changing beliefs is creativity. Challenge yourself to think of new ways to reprogramme yourself, as it's these unexpected and pleasant experiences that have helped me the most.

Dreams

I used to not sleep very well. Not only that, I didn't often have good dreams. They've reduced, but I used to have many scary and strange dreams, depending on what I'm going through in life. Stress makes it worse for me.

It's good. I appreciate them, as they're bringing information into my consciousness that I'm struggling to see. An opening of bs boxes in dreams, if you will. Why am I telling you this? Well, the truth is that most of my bad dreams had one common theme that took me a very long time to recognise: They enacted my belief of powerlessness.

They were bad dreams simply because I believed I couldn't do anything to protect myself. I believed I was helpless, so I didn't have any thoughts on how to help myself. I'd be absolutely terrified, wake up, try to calm myself down, and try to sleep with my lamp on.

The forms of my dreams differed, of course, but the most common ones were of me being attacked by dogs or horses. Sometimes humans and random demons, but the animals were most common. To clarify, I haven't been attacked by an animal in real life, so these are not

memories. Anyway, in the dreams, they'd attack, I'd fall over, too afraid to fight back, they'd harm me in some way, and I'd wake up.

Then I started researching the meanings behind them, and I read somewhere about consciously changing your response in the dreams. I couldn't do this in my dreams because I was too afraid. What I could do, though, was decide that once I woke up, I would take a few minutes to imagine being in the dream again and do something other than freeze.

In fact, what I chose to do was something as unrealistic as it needed to be, to make me feel and be powerful in the face of my danger. So, I'd imagine I have a superpower, or magic, or fighting skills, where I could overpower the danger. I'd equip myself with what I needed to be powerful in my dreams.

Then I would imagine cremating the danger and ending its existence in my mind. I'd thank it for the lesson and take a minute to celebrate, being proud of myself for changing the situation. For empowering myself. Then I'd go back to sleep, feeling proud and powerful.

I did this for months whenever I had a bad dream and woke up. This wasn't every night, just whenever I'd get them. I still do this when I have a bad dream.

And you know what? This really worked. I just had a bad dream last week of a dog attacking me, and instead of freezing, I fought back and stopped it from hurting me. I actually dreamt this. I didn't imagine it after I woke up. Rather, I woke up right after my victory.

Then I did my ritual of cremating the danger and thanking it for the experience. I was incredibly proud of myself and fell straight back to sleep.

So, if your fears are showing in your dreams like mine, consciously changing your response to them from powerless to powerful immediately after waking can help you to change your beliefs and instinct to freeze.

Visualisations

This method is similar to the dreams, as you are imagining something, but it's not related to your dreams. I like to create my own visualisations based on the situation. I know there are a lot of visualisations on the internet that you can follow, though honestly, they never quite hit the spot for me to process my thoughts and emotions the way I needed to.

So, I decided to try a challenge of sitting down for ten minutes and just letting myself visualise whatever I wanted. This is what I meant by creativity. You have to allow yourself to do something different. Something that probably doesn't make sense, and you doubt will help you, but you try it—just in case.

Visualisations were this for me, as I didn't believe in their power. Now, I enjoy them, as my imagination creates some really cool things to process whatever I need to.

I'll give you some examples you can use. Read the paragraph, then put the book down and just imagine it.

See how it feels. For most of my visualisations, I like to imagine I'm in an empty white room. It helps me focus on exactly what I need to, rather than the background. You can imagine being wherever you'd be most comfortable.

I know that a lot of people recommend physically writing something on paper and burning it. It just doesn't work for me. Instead, having something, anything, weird and unrealistic included in my visualisations makes them powerful in processing my internal pains and challenges.

For the first visualisation, I want you to imagine you're standing in an empty white room, looking at yourself, with about six feet of distance between you. This version is the afraid, frozen version of you who doesn't know you can respond to fears better. You take one step forwards. The other you cowers, tucking your head and trying to hide.

You continue walking forwards while the other you becomes more afraid, tears running down your face. Once you reach yourself, you embrace yourself in your powerful safety. You cradle yourself and say, "It's okay, you don't have to keep being afraid." The other you stops crying and looks at you surprised. Next you say, "You *are* powerful." The other you is shocked.

You continue to tell yourself everything you need to hear to believe you are not powerless anymore. Every time you do, the other you changes. The face relaxes and the body opens. You stop cowering and start standing

tall. Eventually, you hug yourself in return and repeat the statements you've made, fully believing them.

Then finally, your bodies, still embraced, merge into one complete being. Aware of your power.

For the second visualisation, I want you to imagine you're in an empty white room. You have a pen in your hand and the ability to write in the air while the words materialise and hover. An interactive whiteboard of sorts.

Now, I want you to draw a line from the middle of your chest forwards, to about a foot in front of you. The line materialises in a bright red. At the end of the line, I want you to write in the air, "I am powerless against all fears and dangers." Draw a circle around it. It materialises in the same red, and you read it a few times.

Gauge the strength of your belief in that statement.

Next, a foot to the right of that belief, I want you to write in the air, "I am powerful against all fears and dangers," with a circle around it. It materialises in bright red. You read it a few times, allowing yourself the possibility of it being true.

Then you draw a line attaching this new belief to the middle of your chest.

Now step back, looking at the two beliefs attached to you, and imagine a huge pair of scissors appearing in your hands, replacing the pen. You look at the red line

attaching yourself to the powerless belief and you cut it. It disintegrates, disconnecting from you.

You are now only connected to the powerful belief.

You walk towards the powerless belief, conjure a cotton bag in your hands, and stuff the circle and words into the bag. You tie it, put the bag on the ground, and set it on fire. You watch it for a few minutes. It is engulfed in flames, eventually turning to ash.

You collect the ashes in a container, close the lid, and cradle it. You grieve the death of this belief and how it served you for so long.

Then, when you're ready, you walk to a hatch that's appearing on your right. You open it, put in the ashes, watch them leave and imagine them flying out of your right ear. Gone. Forever.

You walk back to standing in front of your powerful belief and relish in this new connection.

EMDR

Eye Movement Desensitisation and Reprocessing (EMDR) is a psychotherapy used to help people process serious trauma. This is a therapy used for people with strong trauma, though I personally have created a different way to use it. The main basis of the method is moving your eyes side to side, while simultaneously thinking about the topic you are struggling with. This is typically done by following someone waving their hand side to side or

watching a video of a dot moving from side to side on a screen. You can't just watch the dot and zone out, though. You must truly focus.

I share this method tentatively and stress that this is not medical advice of any kind. I advise you to thoroughly do your research before you move forwards, as EMDR can be quite triggering. I won't go into using EMDR for healing, as that is something I'd like to explore in volume two. You can hire an EMDR therapist if you'd like to explore traditional EMDR more deeply.

However, in this book, I would like to introduce the idea of using EMDR for beliefs. This is not something that's been professionally recommended to me by anyone; it's simply something I developed for myself while I was doing EMDR for my memories.

If you've never done EMDR before and try this method, I can't guarantee what your experience will be like. I tried this after around six sessions of EMDR, working on different topics. I would like to share it with you, though, because it's now the main way that I quickly and easily change my beliefs.

I pick an EMDR simulation video on YouTube, put it on full screen on my iPad, and pause it at the beginning. Then I close my eyes and fully think about and activate the belief I would like to change. For example, let's say it's, "I am always powerless." I chant it in my head, open my eyes, and play the video.

While chanting it, I watch the dot going side to side. It can take a few minutes to relax into it. Sometimes I have

one or multiple memories come forwards that created the belief. I watch them and wait for anything else to come up. When nothing else comes forwards, I consciously chant and affirm the new belief I want instead.

So, I change it to, "I am always powerful." I repeat it, while following the dot, until I feel the shift and really believe this. Next, I stop the video, close my eyes, and allow myself to process. Then I get on with my day.

If there are any other negative beliefs I want to change, I do the same process with those. And that's it. That's the process I use to change the subconscious beliefs I don't want anymore. This practice works immediately for me, and I feel an instant shift. The number of rounds of EMDR videos (typically three minutes each) changes each time I do this practice; however, it really does work. Sometimes, there are beliefs and memories that take multiple sessions to really take effect, though after just one session, I feel a big shift. Each session should be spaced out by a week in between.

Please use your discernment with this. It is a very powerful form of therapy, and can be quite triggering for some people. It also may not work for everyone. That's why I have guided you through the three main methods I use to change my beliefs here. Usually, one method on its own doesn't work for me. I need a multifaceted approach. I have done all three of these things to work on my belief of powerlessness. That's why it's changing for me. I don't think just one method would have worked as successfully.

Just One Belief

I was once asked what keeps me from backing down in the face of my fears and challenges. At that moment, I didn't have an answer. It took me months to figure it out: I have a resolute belief that I am powerful enough to conquer everything I am afraid of.

This realisation has become a beacon in my life, lighting my way forwards. I feel this is the single belief necessary to face and fight your fears.

Believing in your power is the guiding light that nurtures the other positive beliefs you're seeding—the ones you want to plant deeply in the soil of your mind, allowing them to grow and overpower the fears and negative thoughts that try to control you.

You just need one solid belief to create the rest. You need to believe, with unwavering conviction, that you have the power to do what you want to do. The power to create new positive beliefs and the power to extinguish the harmful ones. You have the power to extinguish the fears you don't want living in your mind anymore.

You must believe that you are more powerful than anything else in your mind. You are more powerful than your opponent, whichever form they take.

That's it. You just need the one. From here, your journey begins.

Thus, if you find yourself freezing before your rats and black cats out of a belief of powerlessness, try the methods

I've suggested, and try creating some new ones to claim your one belief: You are powerful enough to fight your fears and change your reality. Do this so you don't stay frozen. Because frozen in fear means frozen in life.

The power is in you. Always.

To summarise chapter five:

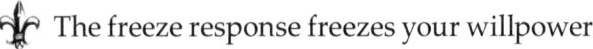 An internal freeze response looks like your mind focussing only on the threat, nothing else, while also either going blank, catastrophising the danger, or knowing but not being able to take action.

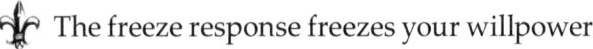 The freeze response freezes your willpower.

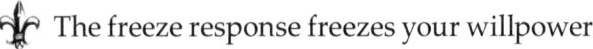 The belief of powerlessness is often the cause of your freeze response.

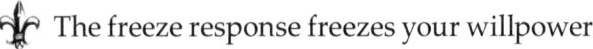 You can change this belief with methods such as conscious dream reactions, visualisations, and EMDR.

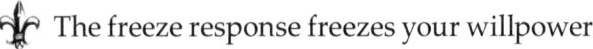 All you need to do is create one resolute belief that you are powerful enough to face and fight your fears.

Call to Action: Try to identify whether you are freezing in response to any of your rats. Are your dreams showing you a message of powerlessness? When you experience the next one, can you change the narrative for yourself?

Chapter Six

Running

The running response is the second way you have been responding to your rats (your unconscious permanent internal fears) and black cats (your amplified dangers) thus far. It's easy to understand what running away from a physical danger is, because you are, of course, physically running and moving away.

This is more difficult to identify with internal dangers because the response takes multiple forms. Internal running is best understood as every action you take that freezing, facing, and fighting isn't.

With every decision taken, the intention is to create distance between you and the black cat, sometimes the rat, whether you realise you're doing it or not.

I've seen this response generally fall into two main categories: avoiding the danger or denying the fear

and danger. There may be other ways you are running away from your internal fears and dangers, though understanding these categories will help you to recognise potential behaviour patterns so you can gain the knowledge you need to understand yourself and your fears in your fear-facing journey.

Avoiding the Danger

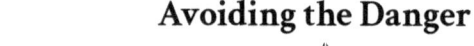

The first form of running is avoiding the black cat. You try to survive by shifting your position away from the danger that stalks in your mind, convinced that constant movement will keep you safe.

Every thought and action is focussed on creating distance with the amplified danger because you believe that running is your lifeline.

Say you have the fear of conflict. Avoiding this danger means rarely instigating or engaging in conflict. This is done by actions like being the pacifier to conflicts you see between others or physically walking away from arguments. In the latter situation, you are physically running away as well as internally.

The conflict, whether it be verbal or physical, makes you feel uncomfortable and unsafe. You believe it's a threat to you, likely because of past experiences. It may even be linked to the fear of being alone and losing a relationship because of conflict. So, you'd rather keep connections with people that are not based on honesty. You'd rather brush your issues under the rug.

That, honestly, is a preference I detest. Brushing things under the rug is not something I appreciate or respect at all, instead using it as a way to judge someone's character (further explored in chapter thirteen). I believe it demonstrates a lack of integrity, authenticity, and courage. It's also delusional to believe you can live in a reality where issues within a relationship, both mistakes and intentional harm, can be easily left in the past and forgotten without them festering.

They can't. Anytime someone feels wronged by another and doesn't directly communicate it to address it, it rots inside of them, and then blows up in the future at some point. Yes, there are certain relationships where it is more difficult to not brush issues under the rug, such as professional ones, and there is a situation for everything. However, no matter the context, it becomes damaging. Fear of conflict would contribute to someone choosing to brush issues under the rug in their attempt to avoid the danger they fear, i.e., conflict.

This is a quintessential black cat. It's a threat that has been highly amplified to the point that you can't see black from white anymore. Yes, conflict can sometimes be uncomfortable from the heated emotions and the chance of losing a relationship. However, it's not a danger to you in any sense at all, especially if you learn to consciously harness the power of it.

Instead of being afraid of conflict and avoiding it, you can see it as an ally in your endeavour of only keeping authentic relationships, if that is something you wish to have and do. You can see that it's an excellent test of character, to observe how people engage in conflict with you, how they act when they lose their temper, and what truths are revealed. Are they willing to work past their defensiveness to move forwards? Do they hold a grudge against you for raising the issue?

Then, based upon these answers, you can make a decision whether this person deserves your trust and respect and whether it's a healthy relationship you want to continue or not.

Conscious conflict actually empowers you. Being afraid of it limits you, like so many other rats. That's why I see them as real dangers to you.

They limit the quality of your experience of life.

Therefore, avoidance feels like safety, but it's a trap. By avoiding every amplified danger, you avoid growth—the chance to become the strongest, happiest version of you.

Progress doesn't come from running away from what challenges you, after all.

Denying the Existence of the Fear and Danger

The second form of running is denying the existence of fear and danger. The first was focussed on how you respond to

the amplified danger, whereas this is about your response to both the fear and the danger.

Running away from a fear is denying that you're afraid. You actively convince yourself it doesn't exist and you're not living from it, meaning you believe all your thoughts, decisions, and actions are coming from a clear-headed space, free from fear.

You could argue that it's possible people just don't know that they're afraid. They're not denying its existence; they simply aren't aware. I counter that fear is such a strong, painful, and shocking experience that it's highly unlikely you could be afraid and not know it. Yes, there is the argument that when you've been living a life of internal fear, you struggle to identify it because it's all you've ever known.

That's not to say that you're completely unaware of it, though. You are. It's alerting you to a danger to your survival, after all. Instead, you're denying its existence every time you get a clue that it's there.

In a sense, the fear becomes a bs box—an internal blind spot—for you. Or rather, you make it into one.

There are varying reasons why you'd do this. Most of them will have the common denominator of not wanting to sacrifice something you value because you admit you're afraid. What do I mean by this?

Well, imagine there's a role you always wanted to try in your sports team. But your coach never allowed it. They didn't even consider it. You respect your coach, but they didn't think about your happiness when making their

decision. You're afraid, though, because you don't want to think badly about them. You don't want to see them as less than perfect and pop your bubble of believed safety. You're afraid of ruining your relationship with them by believing they don't value your happiness as much as they should.

So, you deny the existence of your fear and danger. You don't let yourself admit there is a threat to your happiness in the form of your coach. You don't admit that you're afraid of losing them by admitting your truth or that you're afraid of disappointing them. You also don't admit that you're afraid of losing the future happiness they will deny. So instead, you continue living by their rules, never advocating for yourself, or by giving up quickly and losing yourself in the process because you value your current believed safety bubble over honesty and your true happiness.

This form of running happens when you deny that you're afraid, so you can stay in your current situation and the suffering existing underneath. But you're terrified of losing the joy you've been living in above it.

You've been averting your gaze because you believe it will keep you safe, when in reality, your current situation is what's hurting you now. You've been trying to avoid pain, while living in pain. This means your actions haven't kept you safe at all. Yes, they've kept you away from what you believe is a grave danger to you, but that belief has not given enough weight to your current suffering, which is likely more painful than what the black cat could ever inflict on you.

There is the argument that you'd rather stay with the suffering you know than something worse and unknown. I argue this comes from the safety in fear and fearful comfort explored in chapter two. This is the killer comfort blanket enveloping you, convincing you to not care about the suffering it's causing. You don't benefit from believing it, though, and I hope I am convincing you otherwise.

Now, what would it look like to not deny your fear and danger?

First, you would begin by not looking away anymore and instead accepting their existence. Continuing the example above, you'd have to begin by acknowledging your pain to yourself and admitting that you're not happy right now. You'd then have to figure out which fears were stopping you from acknowledging that pain. You'd face them.

After this, you'd fight the fears by taking action to stop living in them. In this instance, you would calmly communicate everything with your coach, tell them what you've been experiencing, and what your needs are to continue being in the team. Then, based on their response, you move forwards.

Running away from your rats and black cats, no matter how you do it, doesn't actually take you anywhere. That's the thing you need to realise.

The Pain of Running

Both freezing and running responses cause harm, but the running response is more *deceptively* damaging, because running feels like action. You're doing something—putting in time, energy, and focus to respond to the perceived danger. And when you're taking action, it's easy to convince yourself that you're solving the problem. After all, you're not just standing still. You're moving. You're doing something. How could that not be helping?

But your choice to run from your fears and amplified dangers isn't helping you. It's hurting you. Your actions haven't ended your suffering. They haven't resolved the fear. They haven't changed anything. You're still living in anxiety, still trapped in the same cycle of avoidance. The only thing that's changed is that you've exhausted yourself in the process.

Running exhausts you. It drains your resources—your time, energy, and focus—on an endeavour that will never succeed. You pour everything you have into escaping, only to stay in the same state of fear and suffering.

You're not intentionally trying to sabotage yourself. But you are. And the self-sabotage of running has no limits. You sabotage yourself by making decisions out of internal fear that are intended to take you away from something you believe could hurt you. You believe you'll struggle to survive, when the pain, in reality, will likely be medium to minimum. There's no question about your survival, and

all the experiences will lead to unprecedented growth and transformation for you.

The sabotage is to your potential because it limits everything you could be and experience just to stay exactly where you are—all to keep something that hasn't been fully serving and satisfying you in the first place.

Say you have the fear of disappointment. You don't want to take a chance on something because you're afraid you'll be let down, likely from past experiences. But then you meet someone. A person you didn't imagine could exist. They are practically made to complement you as a romantic partner.

But you're afraid it might not work out and you'll experience that dreaded disappointment you're trying to avoid. In your mind, the disappointment is the worst pain you could experience because you've amplified the severity of it so much in your head. That danger amplification is so much louder than your excitement and hope in having your wants and needs fulfilled that it almost overpowers it.

Almost. It almost overpowers it. It doesn't completely snuff it out, though. The fear doesn't kill that inherent part of you. It can't. And you shouldn't let it.

Why not just stop running away from your fear and take a chance? On you and your happiness. Okay, so you're afraid of disappointment. But imagine the possibility of what you could experience if you moved forwards with this. What if your dreams could come true?

Don't you want to find out who you are without fear?

99

Facing your fears isn't just about conquering them—it's about finding yourself in the process. By facing what scares you, you uncover the parts of yourself that have been buried under avoidance, fear, and self-doubt. You're not just removing obstacles—you're rediscovering who you are and who you can become.

More than that, you're giving yourself a chance, a real chance, at improving your experience of life. At making it into the most satisfying, peaceful, and pleasurable it can possibly be. You rob yourself of this without fighting for it.

Do you really want to keep depriving yourself of happiness by running away?

The Power to Run

However you choose to run—whether you are avoiding, denying existence, or anything else—you are doing it because, deep down, you believe it is the best way to avoid pain. This belief is what separates the instinct to flee from the instinct to freeze. You freeze because you believe you are utterly powerless. But when you run, it's because you feel a single power within you, and you are using that power to save yourself.

The power to run is fueled by the belief that you can escape the rats and black cats. The path is clear in your mind—possible, practical, and within reach. Each step is fueled by the conviction that running is your only helpful ability. Your sole chance at survival.

More than that, you don't believe you have the power to aim for anything beyond basic and temporary safety. Survival becomes your only goal because it feels like the only reality you can achieve.

However, as explored in chapters five and nine, this is not the only power at your disposal. You can earn more power for yourself—primarily the power to defend yourself and keep yourself safe.

Internal Safety

I think internal safety is an interesting concept, as we aren't taught much about how to cultivate, nurture, and protect it. I think most people imagine internal safety to be an environment without any dangers. A safe haven where no one can internally hurt you.

I don't think that's possible, in the same way it isn't possible for our physical environments. How do we feel safe physically, then, and can we extend those practices to our internal world?

I think we can. The way I see it, there are two main methods to keep yourself physically safe that can be used here. There are more; though, I'd like to focus on these two for now.

The first is an awareness of what does and doesn't pose a threat to you. This awareness is your first safety mechanism, built into your instincts, such as knowing when to back away from someone who looks like a threat

or has equipped themselves with something that poses a threat, like a gun.

With your internal world, this awareness is then related to your internal dangers. Knowing them and building the skill to objectively assess how much of a real threat this thing poses to you. Judging it by how much damage it's likely to cause, not the worst pain you could imagine inflicted. That way you can make an informed decision on how to respond, instead of acting out of constant panic.

That's what I've found so useful about the fear-facing journey, because this is a skill I have had to build, and am continually working on honing. Now I assess the internal danger I had amplified, take myself out of a fearful state, and really question my beliefs regarding this threat to my survival. It usually isn't a threat. It's either a figment of my imagination and beliefs and didn't hurt me at all when I experienced it, like fear of failure, or the pain I experienced as an aftermath was challenging but character building.

How you can hone this skill is what this whole book is about. Part one gives you an awareness of real dangers— the rats—that have been harming you, that you were likely blind to. This gives you the ability to compare the pain you're afraid of to the pain you're already experiencing.

Part two shows you how to break down your fears into different strands, so you realise there are many interconnected threats you're believing in right now. This awareness shows you how to target one fear or amplified danger at once.

Part three explains how you've been unknowingly responding to your fears so you can understand them in a different way and then catch your behaviour patterns in action. Once you've caught them, you can change how you respond to the fears, i.e., by consciously not freezing and running.

Part four dives deep into some topics related to the causes of your reactions and your beliefs about the dangers themselves. This shows a perspective that's likely different from your own and demonstrates an analysis of your fears and amplified dangers. You can build your awareness of your real internal threats by sifting through the rats you have and dissecting the black cats to understand whether the harm they threaten is even something to fear.

Finally, part five gives you techniques to snap yourself out of your fear response, allowing you to start thinking clearly again. So you see, the fear-facing journey explored in this whole book has been targeted towards giving you a chance to earn the power of knowledge, the skill of internal threat detection, and personal awareness that will be your first mechanism to keep yourself safe.

As the first awareness is about the fears and dangers themselves, the second is the awareness of your own capabilities in the face of danger. Most of the time, all you need to feel safe is knowing that you can keep yourself safe—physically and internally. That's why martial arts and boxing can be such an empowering experience. It gives people a skill, a fighting chance, to defend themselves.

There are layers to this personal awareness, though. The first is knowing what moves you can make before a threat, which is all about fighting your fears (explored in volume two). The second is an awareness of how much pain you can and are willing to experience. Internally speaking, how hard are you willing to be hit to fight your fears?

I find this so interesting because it is less explored. Physically, when someone is a skilled fighter, or even a trainee fighter, they begin with a high willingness to be hurt. That pain is not something they are afraid of or is holding them back from what they want to do. It's simply a side effect they accept. They'll have the fight, be injured, heal afterwards, and then do it again.

Whereas, internally, I feel that sometimes the pain is taken so seriously by people there is no willingness at all to experience any pain to gain something better and greater. That's why you're running away from it. However, I put to you, is it really so bad that you've subjected yourself to a life of pain, fearful comfort, freezing, and running? I very much doubt it.

Isn't one form of strength a willingness to experience pain for something that is important to you? To not crack under the pressure and torment of something that is threatening what you love and value the most?

I truly encourage you to grow your willingness to experience temporary internal pain in varying degrees of severity for your growth, peace, and freedom, as that's

likely what you need to do to stop running. It's how you keep yourself safe from real threats to your internal self.

How do you do this? Well, for me, it becomes an incredibly easy decision when I consider and connect with the alternative and how that's not an option for me. Living through my rats for the rest of my life is something I'm genuinely afraid of, so I'll do what I need to do and accept the pain necessary to not make that into a reality. By consciously making something else more important than the temporary internal pain, your willingness expands.

To end this chapter, freezing and running are the responses you have likely unknowingly been activating for your rats and black cats. There are varying reasons for this, but what matters most is that you can change your responses and choose to face and fight those fears instead.

To summarise chapter six:

Running responses are actions taken by you to create distance between yourself, the rats, and the black cats.

The first form of running is avoiding the amplified danger, and the second is denying the existence of the fear and danger.

You are running away from a pain you're afraid of, while living in the pain you're experiencing right now. So, your current actions aren't keeping you safe.

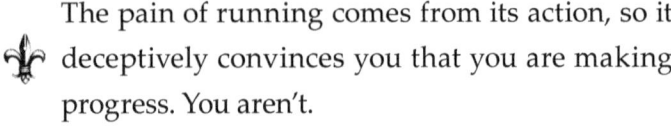 The pain of running comes from its action, so it deceptively convinces you that you are making progress. You aren't.

Instead, you are sabotaging yourself, your happiness, and growth.

The main reason people run is because they believe that is the only power they have.

People can stop running and keep themselves internally safe by honing the skill of internal threat detection and personal awareness for themselves.

Call to Action: Can you identify whether you are running from any of your rats and black cats? Is it the first method, or second?

Chapter Seven

The Effect of Fear

The final chapter of part three is focussed on facing how the strand of fear (explored in chapter four) you've chosen has been affecting you, what you believe the consequences of experiencing it are, and then stepping back to build an awareness on what is likely to happen instead.

So, do you truly know yourself? Or do you only know the version that's afraid?

There is a difference. A significant one. The permanently afraid and panicked version is not the real you.

The truth is, you can't find your true self if you only know the afraid version. To understand your real self, you first need to identify your scared self. This is easier to recognise because it's the current version you've been

living as. It's also fueled by fear and anxiety, which means you can feel it to identify it.

To do this, you'll be looking at how this particular fear or strand of fear has been affecting you. In a tangible sense, how has this fear influenced you and your life?

This isn't just about feeling frightened. I want you to identify exactly how the fear has shaped your lifestyle. On a daily, monthly, even yearly basis, what do you choose to do or not do because of this rat? This will give you clear evidence of the actions and behaviour patterns of your scared self.

By directly searching for everything you've been doing out of a fear response, and questioning it and yourself, you'll be able to reflect and choose different responses in the future. You'll be able to compare what you have been doing out of fear with what you want to do instead, and what you will do when you live without fear.

I have outlined below how I like to organise the actions, though you may adjust this outline to fit your needs:

Category One - Mistakes

The first category of effects your strand may have had on you is mistakes made from fear. This encompasses everything you've done while afraid, that you wouldn't have done if you weren't.

Focus only on those actions connected to the specific strand you've been working on through this process. Think

about all the times in your life you've done something because you were afraid of that specific strand. What did you do and why? Keep noting them on your mind map as you remember. Don't force yourself to recall them all at once, as it's unlikely you'll be able to. Rather, starting this task will allow your subconscious to search through your past for the mistakes and remind you over time.

You've probably lived your life thinking these decisions were from a well-considered, reasonable, thoughtful place—but in reality, they stemmed from an anxious state. It can be tough to really consider the possibility that you've been making decisions, and mistakes, with fear as your greatest contributor. Try not to be too hard on yourself.

Blame the nasty rats instead. It's their fault.

After you've gathered your fear-driven mistakes, what do you do with this information? Well, the first thing I would do is look at each one intently and see if, or rather how, I can rectify them. What can I do to apologise and fix my mistakes, so I can move forwards without making them into a regret?

If you identify mistakes not made from fear in this process, great. Create a separate list for yourself.

These mistakes will split into different categories themselves, namely ones you can rectify and ones you can't. For the ones you can, make a decision on how you'd like to do that and take immediate action. It doesn't have to be anything too grand or time consuming. Rather, it's about taking ownership for your fear-driven mistakes, and acknowledging you wouldn't have done that if you weren't afraid. And then asking, if it's a person, for a chance to see you without fear.

Continuing the fear of disappointment example from the last chapter, say this dream partner approached you and showed their interest. Out of your fear, you rejected them. Maybe even insulted them. You made a mistake, though, because you deprived yourself and hurt them in the process. So, after you realised this was simply rat-driven behaviour and would like to rectify this mistake, you contacted them, asking if they could talk. You met up, apologised for your behaviour, and explained it was simply out of fear and is something you don't want to continue living in. And now you're asking them to give you another chance.

Their response doesn't matter, so much as the fact that you took action to fix your mistake. They may accept or reject you. They may insult you in return. Their reaction just shows you a reflection of them. What matters is that you did something with the knowledge you've gained in this fear-facing journey to make your life better.

After all, that's the true value of information. It helps you take action in your life. The knowledge helps you move forwards with your actions. Collecting knowledge on its own doesn't necessarily do that. I'm hoping that the topics explored in my books will help you move forwards in your life with your actions created from the knowledge you've learned. They provide assistance for your actions; they're not knowledge simply for learning.

You must get creative to rectify your mistakes, as I can't list out every single way you can do this. That's something only you can do. It's not incredibly difficult, though, and usually takes the form of communicating an apology and ownership of your rat-driven mistakes.

Category Two - Missed Opportunities

The second category involves recognising the opportunities you've missed. What didn't you or haven't you done, simply because you were/are intimidated or afraid? What do you regret not taking a chance on?

You might find this category easier to identify than the first. I've found I can never seem to move on from missed opportunities the way I can with my mistakes. With missed opportunities, I always have this nagging thought at the back of my head, constantly asking: *Did I just miss out on something great? Did my fear stop me from leaping into the unknown, missing out on something incredible, that could have changed me and my life forever?*

With missed opportunities, you can never quite move on from what could have been if you had just been brave enough to jump.

So, gather all your missed chances regarding the strand of fear you're facing and create two lists. The first list is for those chances that are gone for good. You must accept that they're lost. The second are those that are still within your

reach. You haven't missed out on them yet but will if you don't take action.

Allow me to demonstrate the difference between the two. Say you are a university student, and there's an internship opportunity you would love to attend. But you're afraid. You believe you won't get it because there's too much competition, and they're all better than you. There's nothing you can offer the company, so there's no point in trying. So you don't apply, the deadline passes, and you miss out. This is a missed opportunity that is gone for good. You can't go back to it.

Whereas, an opportunity that is still within your reach would be another internship opportunity that is currently taking applications and you still have time to apply. Or maybe you're applying for graduate roles now, and there is one in particular you would love to be a part of. You're still afraid, though, and are considering missing it.

Now, review the lists you have created. Look at the first category—at what your fear has already caused you to miss out on in your life. Truly think about the loss of opportunity. Next, look at the second category and think about what else the rat wants you to miss—the chances it's trying to deny you.

Look at how your rat has sabotaged you, and how it is still trying to do the same thing. Decide to never let your rats hold you back again. Never let them make you miss an opportunity again. You have a list of ripe chances right in front of you, begging you to take action towards them.

Review them and their reasonableness. Check whether it's just your rats holding you back from them, or whether there is further logic to consider. Asking a trusted friend or advisor to review them with you might help you to discern which opportunities are ones you're not going to let yourself miss out on. You're not going to add them to the first category.

Now take action towards them, whatever you need to do—an email or conversation. Applying for something. Booking that programme or holiday. Step forwards despite the strand of fear because you're more afraid of something else.

Fear of your rats, yes. But fear of another regret. That is more powerful than any of the fears trying to deprive you of another great thing. It doesn't matter if you don't get it. What matters is that you don't regret not trying.

By clearly laying these two categories out, you can distinguish between your fearful and fearless self because you have evidence of their actions and behaviour. This starts building your awareness of your scared self to keep you safe from your fears.

Fearless isn't Reckless

I'd like to take a minute to explore fearlessness. Being fearless is something I don't think is possible, to be honest. I think the goal is more becoming consciously fearful and a skilled unconscious-fear facer and fighter.

Being fearless is not the same as being reckless, however. Recklessness involves acting without thought, ignoring potential risks, and not considering the safety of yourself and others.

Fearlessness, on the other hand, means that unconscious and unhelpful fear no longer influences your decision-making process. This doesn't imply that you're not making informed and thoughtful choices—just that you're not unnecessarily afraid as you make them.

Yes, there are moments in life when fearlessness and recklessness come together. Sometimes, being reckless is exactly what you need to take the greatest leaps of your life.

Sometimes, you need to stop thinking and just jump.

That's not all the time, though. It's not even most of the time. That's why, as you become more aware of your fears, dangers, and yourself, I encourage you to use this to make conscious, well-informed decisions, instead of thoughtless ones. This helps move you forwards in the direction you actually want to go.

Belief of Consequence

So far in part three, we've explored how the rats have been affecting you with the freezing and running responses, as well as your mistakes and missed opportunities. Now, we're going to look to the future. Or rather, your imagined catastrophised future.

What exactly do you believe will happen if your fear becomes reality? Explore this deeply, following every possibility to the end. I want you to face the absolute worst-case scenario of this fear.

Doing this exercise might feel uncomfortable, as if you're experiencing your fear firsthand. In some ways, you are. But more importantly, you're also uncovering all the assumptions you have about this rat and black cat materialising. The chain of events is rooted in a set of beliefs—a complex belief system—that you're likely unaware of.

Not everything you believe is true. Most are probably false exaggerations based on unhealed trauma or missing information.

Let's walk you through an example. Say you have a deep fear of disappointing your parents. It would pain you very deeply if that happened, and this fear stops you from doing some things that you truly want to do. This fear was likely created by your parents as a child to compel you not to do anything that would disappoint them. But you have also likely amplified the danger to the worst-case scenario, such as your parents disowning you for the most minor situation. You are likely missing information here, and if you were to have a serious conversation with your parents about disappointing them, they may say that's never a possibility. Or that the disappointment was something they used in their parenting, and it was never meant to affect you as an adult.

Or maybe they were serious about it, and what you imagined to be the worst was realistic. Well, not to play the devil's advocate here, as they've made their boundaries clear, but you have the right to do the same with yours. Their boundaries are focussed on their happiness, not mutual happiness. And you've been living by those, sacrificing your own. This would be a situation in which you would carefully navigate the fear to decide whether you want to stay where you are—in pain and fear—or whether you want to move forwards.

That's why you need to see exactly what each belief of consequence is—so you can consciously evaluate what you really are afraid of and see how unlikely most of it is. Beliefs are further explored in chapter eight.

Timeline of Events

If imagining living through your fears to understand your beliefs feels overwhelming, write a fictional story instead. You don't have to engage in detailed world-building or character creation, unless you want to. The important thing is to draft a timeline for a story, detailing what you believe must occur for your fear to become a reality for the character. What events make the threat real? Then map out exactly how the fear hurts the character. Afterwards, develop a sequence of events based on your beliefs about what happens to the character once the fear materialises.

What specifically do you think is going to happen? Plot it out with your character. Do this by repeatedly asking

yourself, "And then what happens?" Keep going further with, "What's next?" until you reach the end of the story. Stop when there's nothing left to happen.

By doing this, by outlining the entire sequence step by step, you can see the complete picture. You can clearly see what you're afraid of. No blind spots of consequence.

Using the story from above, I have listed below an example:

- You do the thing you wanted to do, like change career paths.

- You go home to tell your parents.

- Your parents become enraged, immediately lose their temper, shouting at you and insulting you.

- They tell you that they are very disappointed to have you as their child.

- You are upset but keep trying to explain yourself.

- They don't listen and kick you out of their home instead.

- They walk you to the door and disown you as their child.

- You leave, never go back to see them again, and they never reach out to you.

You live the rest of your life without your parents' love.

Reason of Consequence

For each consequence or step of the timeline, it's important to determine the belief that created that outcome, and why you hold that belief. The best approach is to write it down beside or beneath the respective step. Use the following format:

"Next, I believe [consequence] will happen, because [insert reason]."

Why do you believe what you believe? What are the specific reasons? The reasons behind your beliefs may repeat or be different. They could be based on memories or simply be beliefs you've copied from someone else. Figuring them out will take time and won't likely be completed in one sitting.

That's perfectly fine; take your time to reflect. This process is more about internal exploration than merely jotting things down. It's important not to rush and potentially overlook the true cause. This process may also be triggering to you, because this is where you are opening bs boxes—your internal blind spots—and seeing things you've ignored for a long time.

It can be very difficult to accept these internal truths. You're not alone, as I've also done this a lot, and other people are doing it with you. Just remember how incredible

a journey you've chosen to go on by facing and fighting your internal fears.

Let me demonstrate this activity using a couple examples:

"Next, I believe my parents will lose their temper and start shouting at me, because this is how they've blown up in the past, so I know they aren't willing to calm themselves down. I also believe they don't care about my happiness or reasons for why I changed my job, and will take my actions as a personal attack."

"Next, I believe my parents will tell me that they are very much disappointed to have me as their child, because they've made it clear that they'll only love me if I'm doing what they approve of. I don't believe they are willing to accept me for wanting different things, and the real me isn't good enough to be loved and accepted by them."

In both examples, I have mixed the reasons for belief to be both memories and beliefs themselves. Yours will likely be similar. Sometimes one specific memory will stick out; sometimes there will be multiple. Sometimes what you believe won't make sense to you or may hurt you to see. That's okay. Just write it down. We're about to question it now.

A Court Hearing for Fear and Belief

The final part of this chapter is to now logically question your beliefs of consequence and the reasons behind them.

This is with the intention of realising what is a probable scenario, not what is the worst case your rat has created.

It may be helpful to do this exercise with someone who doesn't share the same fear as you. You could swap timelines and challenge each other's beliefs and reasons, then discuss and compare what you both do and don't believe is likely or true. Give evidence to each other, opposing their beliefs. This is a great way to find missing information.

Doing this task with a trusted friend will be the best way to do it, as you need someone who will help you challenge your beliefs. You don't want to do it alone where you are affirming those beliefs instead of challenging them or even completing this task with a friend who will affirm them.

You need to make it clear with the person you choose that their role is to challenge your beliefs logically, never insult you personally for having them. Same goes for you. This also isn't a place to get emotional while diving into past experiences, as that won't help you challenge your beliefs of consequence. It will fuel you to affirm them instead. So, try to focus on the task at hand. If you find yourself struggling, take a break and come back to it when you both feel calm and focussed. Impartial.

Essentially, you're allowing your fears an opportunity to prove themselves and earn their right to live inside you for the first time.

Not all your beliefs and fears will be irrational. Some of them might have parts worth keeping. The goal isn't to

be inhumanly fearless but rather to make an intentional decision about which fears can stay. You simply aren't blindly staying afraid anymore.

Imagine this questioning process as a trial for your fears and beliefs .

While they can't speak for themselves like a person can, they still exist and can be questioned to help you reach a fair and informed decision. Question every belief you've noted in your timeline. Thoroughly. I've provided some sample questions below to get you started, but ultimately, your advocacy is your own. Feel free to ask any questions that need answering. You are the one answering them, after all.

Question One - Is this a reasonable belief?

This question is one that will absolutely be helpful to utilise a friend, as you will likely struggle to form arguments for why it's not a reasonable belief to hold.

When reviewing the belief from a logical perspective rather than an emotional one, does it seem reasonable? Is there enough evidence supporting it? Is it based on the balance of probabilities?

The balance of probabilities is the standard of proof used in United Kingdom civil law cases, where the court must be satisfied that an event is more likely to have occurred than not. It's often described as a "fifty-one percent chance." In the legal context, it's used for

past events. Whereas, for your fear-imagined situation, you can adapt its use to determine whether the belief of consequence has a fifty-one percent chance of happening. If it doesn't, then give yourself permission to rule against its probability. You don't need to go as far as proving it beyond reasonable doubt, which is the standard of proof for criminal law cases. You just need enough to realise that it's not a reasonable belief to hold. And even if it does happen, it's not worth you permanently being afraid of it.

Based on the evidence you and your friend have gathered for—and against—its reasonableness, make a decision on whether it's a belief you'd like to keep or not. Ideally, the evidence you have collected to disprove it should have done its job. If not, you can do further work to change your beliefs, as explored in chapter five. You don't necessarily need to have enough evidence to completely disprove what you believe and are afraid will happen, but just enough to realise that it's not reasonable or realistic, and you have amplified it. This in turn should make you less afraid of it.

Question Two - Is this belief helpful, hindering, or harmful?

How does this belief influence you? Does it help you live a better, happier life? Is it informative? Or does it cause anxiety without any real standing? Is it overwhelmingly

negative and causing chaos in your internal residence and life?

This question is more closed than open. By this, I mean the answer will be either helpful, hindering, or harmful. Trying to justify all three won't help you to move forwards. It might be all three, but which one is it the most? Is it worth keeping something you think is helpful, though in reality, it is harming you more?

Not really, as ideally most, with the goal of eventually reaching all—if this is possible—of your beliefs should be helping you be the person you want to be and experience life the way you want to. Personally, this is one of my greatest considerations when deciding how I move forwards with something, such as responding to fear and changing my beliefs.

Question Three - Did you miss something?

Finally, considering what led to your belief, was it based on a partial truth? Is there information you don't know, or are refusing to see, that could change your belief entirely? Are you open to adjusting your viewpoint to acknowledge this missing information?

Doing this task with your close friend will be particularly useful here, as they may point out some information that you weren't aware of. Or maybe they can ask you questions with the goal of uncovering what you don't know, such as, "What evidence do you have for this

being true?", "Do you know the reason they said that?" and, "Have you asked them about this?"

Speaking to your friend will be the first part of this, though really the greater part is going directly to the source of your belief, if it's a person, and asking for more information. Try finding what you're missing. Understand their reasoning and the whole context. You probably don't know everything.

If you overlooked something and have now gained new insights, has your belief shifted? Has this then affected your timeline?

If you didn't learn anything new, rather your belief was affirmed, how would you like to go forwards with this? You can keep it, of course. But did the evidence gathered earlier give you enough information to not amplify it as much?

With this type of questioning, you are challenging your beliefs and giving yourself the chance to see what is a probable reality for you, and whether that is something you'll be willing to experience anyway.

And in this, you have built a new form of awareness to add to your skills of internal safety. One that will help you respond to your rats and black cats consciously, and hopefully, start dissipating them instead of amplifying them, in turn, reducing the pain of fear you have been living with.

To conclude chapter seven, and end part three, facing how you have been responding to your rats thus far empowers you with the knowledge you need to understand

yourself enough to change those responses. Without this, your efforts to fight your fears may not be as effective, as you simply don't know enough about them.

To summarise:

- You don't know your true self if you only know the afraid version of yourself.

- Build an awareness of how your fear has been affecting you in the past with your mistakes and missed opportunities.

- Take action rectifying those mistakes, and try not to miss out on more opportunities now that you're aware of them.

- Next, explore your beliefs of consequence to build your awareness of what you believe will happen if the fear becomes a reality and why.

- Then question these beliefs to logically figure out how you've amplified your beliefs, which ones are worth keeping, and which ones aren't.

- Asking a close and trusted friend to help you with this process, or doing it together, will help you to see through your fear and question it.

Call to Action: Find a trusted friend to test the process of this chapter and come to an agreement on how you can both support each other best with it.

PART FOUR

Facing
the Why

Chapter Eight

Beliefs

In part four, we're going to be exploring three topics that are essential to understanding why you've been responding to your rats—your unconscious permanent internal fears—the way you have. The first topic is beliefs, which affects more than just your fears. They affect every area of your life.

The second chapter is power, and your beliefs regarding it, which greatly influences whether you freeze, flee, face, or fight your fears. Lastly, we will explore internal needs, your beliefs around them, and whether you're subconsciously afraid of something that is an internal need of yours and deprivation of it is the thing causing you pain.

I will demonstrate how helpful it can be to dive deep into a topic or concept, define it, and break it down into its different forms. We did this with fears in chapter

one, and now will do the same with beliefs, powers, and needs. One reason we can become so overwhelmed and unproductive with personal development is that we struggle to differentiate between the forms of something that are helpful versus those that are hindering or harmful.

Breaking the different forms of fears, beliefs, powers, or anything else down into distinguishable forms makes them more manageable to us, as we can address each one individually, rather than collectively. This empowers us to take direct action to achieve small specific goals, such as changing a negative belief to a positive one.

The best way I can describe this is that each topic in part four is its own wing of the internal residence, and it consists of rooms full of bs boxes - internal blind spots. There's a lot you don't know yet or haven't seen. By opening the bs boxes, you can organise the information into the relevant categories/rooms. Then you know what exists, with what function, and where you've organised it to understand it easily.

I have organised the information in my book based on how I find it easiest to break each internal topic down to understand it. You may find it easiest to understand it differently, and that's okay.

Let's begin. Beliefs are not fleeting thoughts or surface-level ideas. They are deeply ingrained convictions that shape how you see and interact with the world. A belief is an acceptance of something as true or real, often without requiring tangible evidence. It acts as the lens through

which you interpret events, navigate relationships, and perceive your potential.

Beliefs come in many forms, depending on their origins and focus. Some are *personal*, shaped by your experiences and internal reflections. These are the beliefs you hold about yourself—your abilities, strengths, weaknesses, and worth. For example, "I am powerful enough to conquer my fears," and, "I believe I am of low intelligence."

Others are *interpersonal*, influenced by your relationships and interactions. These beliefs reflect how you see others and how you think they see you. Examples of interpersonal beliefs are: "My parents love me unconditionally," and, "I believe that my friend is a manipulative person."

Then there are *impersonal* beliefs, which relate to external systems, forces, or objects. These might include beliefs about the structure of society or the nature of the Universe, such as, "Manchester Trafford Centre is a great place to go shopping," and, "I believe politics is full of liars."

Beliefs can take any shape you allow. You can choose to believe in your strengths and capabilities, or you can choose to believe in your limitations and lack of control. Similarly, you can assign power to yourself, to others, or to external systems.

These beliefs rarely exist in isolation. They intertwine, forming complex systems that reinforce and sustain one another. Together, they guide your thoughts, shape your

perspectives, and ultimately influence your decisions and actions.

In this way, beliefs construct your reality. They determine how you see and navigate the world around you. Most importantly, they shape how you understand and experience your own power—or the absence of it.

Unconscious Beliefs

Beliefs are among the strongest forces that influence you. Negative beliefs hinder and harm you, while positive ones support and uplift. But unconscious beliefs—hidden and numbering in the hundreds or thousands even—affect you without your knowledge.

Unconscious beliefs are those you carry without awareness or deliberate choice. Most of them are formed early in life, not through careful reasoning, but by default. If you're unwilling to challenge them, you instinctively reject anything that contradicts them.

You carry these beliefs much like you carry the rats and black cats, but their presence isn't always obvious. They're like moths, clouding your thoughts with their dust, making it harder to see clearly or navigate beyond the paths they've set for you.

Not all unconscious beliefs are negative, but when they are, their potential for harm is immense. They influence every thought, decision, action, and interpretation. Your negative belief-moths and fear-rats act as filters through

which you see the world. When your mind is overrun with them, you lose clarity, self-control, and a sense of who you are at your core.

These moths then become negative belief systems, which carve rigid routes in your thinking, forcing your reasoning to follow predetermined pathways that only lead to conclusions they dictate.

Instead of helping you, they limit you.

When you can't assess the information you're processing, question its validity, or make objective judgments, you lose more than just basic functionality—you lose the ability to consciously grow and move forwards. Plus, this limitation on your ability to thoroughly question or scrutinise others leaves you vulnerable to manipulation and exploitation.

Let's now dive into two types of unconscious beliefs: imposed and credulous. There are more, such as those embedded with manipulation, though we won't explore them here. This is just to give you a demonstration of how you can dive deep into each subtopic, such as unconscious beliefs.

Imposed

Imposed beliefs are those placed on you by someone else, by a single person or many. These beliefs can take root at any stage of life, from childhood to adulthood. As an adult,

it is generally harder for beliefs to be imposed upon you, as you'll likely naturally question the imposition.

For children, that imposition is more difficult to recognise. For example, as a child, you may have been warned against befriending someone by your parents for your safety. You trusted them and so unconsciously adopted their beliefs that this person was bad news and someone for you to avoid.

It happens when you're told you must believe something, so you do. Intimidation may have played a role, or perhaps you simply weren't ready to question or reject it. Instead, you accepted it. You adopted someone else's truth without examining it for yourself. Not all imposed beliefs are harmful or negative, like the situation above. They are unconscious, though.

Credulous

Credulous beliefs are the ones you take on without a second thought—with no real evidence to back them up.

Unlike imposed beliefs, no one forces these on you. Instead, they're beliefs you absorb from the people around you, without stopping to ask yourself if they actually make sense or align with your values. They'll also be absorbed from your wider environment, such as the media.

For example, imagine you're spending time with your friend who is speaking of someone they hate. Someone you don't personally know. They make many statements

against them and you listen, believing every word. You adopt those beliefs against this person because you trust your friend and are loyal to them. They didn't directly tell you which beliefs to adopt; rather, you absorbed them from them.

This tendency to take on others' convictions without questioning them can come from a desire to belong. You want to feel accepted. You want respect, appreciation, and connection. In that quest, you might find yourself mirroring someone else's beliefs, adopting their truths as your own in the hope that it will bring you closer to them.

Other reasons may be genuine trust and respect in the person you're listening to, a lack of confidence in your ability and right to question them, loyalty, and social survival.

My issue with unconscious beliefs is that we didn't consciously choose them. So the direction they lead us in wasn't chosen, neither was the effect they have on us.

Whether you choose to have negative or positive *conscious beliefs* is based on how you want them to make you feel. Oftentimes, I've found my moths feed my victim mentality. When I'm feeling sorry for myself in a situation, and I am wrapped in the killer comfort blanket, they are keeping me in it. And sometimes, I need a day or two to wallow in self-pity to process those emotions. But then I choose to put a lot of conscious effort into taking off that blanket, not thinking negatively of myself and my situation, and consciously changing my beliefs into positive, empowering ones instead. Because that's how I choose to think and feel.

But when you have *unconscious beliefs*, you haven't chosen them. Not all of them are bad, and many will be positive and helpful. You might even have more positive than negative ones, and you can choose to keep them when you've found them. It's the negative ones that sabotage you, though, and that's what I encourage you to change.

Conscious

Conscious beliefs are those you've intentionally chosen to adopt after assessing them yourself. You were presented with information—either something new or something that challenged what you already believed—and you made the decision to accept it.

In one scenario, you learned something new. That learning led to the creation of conscious beliefs, built on your fresh understanding of a situation. In another, you were open to questioning your existing beliefs. When presented with contrasting information, you deliberated. You either chose to keep the belief you previously held or transformed it into a new conscious belief.

All beliefs—conscious and unconscious—have the power to shape you. But when you allow unconscious or unassessed beliefs to dominate, you let the circumstances that created them shape you without your consent. You become a version of yourself that isn't entirely your own.

Over time, this leaves you vulnerable, shaped more by what you've been subjected to than by your own choices.

Yet, the power to shape yourself is always within your will. You have the ability to create as many conscious beliefs—and belief systems—as you need. You can craft every part of yourself to align with the person you want to be. You can become the version of yourself that brings you the most happiness.

You don't have to live with beliefs that make you miserable. You don't have to hold on to beliefs that cause you suffering. You can change them. By activating your inner power to consciously assess and choose your beliefs, one by one, you shape yourself into something extraordinary. You become the Michelangelo of your own marble, sculpting a life that is better, easier, and happier.

Conscious beliefs, when chosen wisely, help you. They are like ants—small but incredibly strong, intelligent, and organised. They work together in harmony, building a cohesive and functional structure. That is what helpful conscious beliefs can do for you—they grow with you, supporting the life you want to create. And the belief systems they create make it easier for you to reach the destinations you want to reach.

Negative vs. Positive

How do beliefs relate to fears? Well, I believe that fears are born from beliefs. When you believe a danger exists

that is significant enough for you to fear, you quickly or eventually fear it. You become afraid of the possibility of that danger belief becoming your reality.

Moths (negative beliefs) are easy to identify—they are the ones that hinder and harm you. They limit your growth and potential. They keep you feeling damaged or powerless. They hold you back from being the person you truly want to be and living the life you want. Examples of these would be: "I'll always be wrong compared to others," "I'm worthless," and, "Bad things always happen to me."

Positive beliefs, on the other hand, are helpful. They support, nurture, and strengthen you. They internally empower you. Positive beliefs are helpful because they assist you with your goals, such as improving your experience of life. This means when you take control of your ability to create your own beliefs, you can intentionally build positive ones that serve you in all the ways you need. With these beliefs, you can strengthen yourself from the inside out. Examples of these are: "I can overcome every challenge I encounter," "I am worthy of having great friends," and, "I believe in my ability to solve all of my problems."

Beliefs also have the power to reinforce one another, whether they are negative or positive. Based on my experience, moths and rats naturally amplify each other. Whereas, for positive beliefs to reinforce each other, a more conscious effort on my part is required.

While it can be challenging to create new positive beliefs that directly counteract your fears and negative beliefs—especially since those moths often resist change—your core positive beliefs can act as a foundation. They can nurture and support the new beliefs you're trying to build.

What do I mean by core positive beliefs? Like we explored general dangers and strands—specific situational fears coming off the general dangers—you can choose to cultivate one strong general positive belief that you can then create many situational positive beliefs from, a sort of mother of positive beliefs who births child beliefs.

In my experience, putting a lot of effort into solidifying that one mother, a general conscious positive belief, makes it so much easier for me to fight my moths and rats because I have this one thing that I resolutely believe. It's the one belief I need to move forwards before all challenges. And then, this mother can be supported by many children—situational conscious positive beliefs—for the specific situations in my life, and vice versa, the mother keeps empowering the children.

Let me walk you through an example of how you can utilise this for yourself. Say you are struggling facing and fighting your internal fears. A big reason for this may be because you don't believe you have the power to do so.

If you consciously cultivate one strong mother of "I am powerful enough to conquer all of my fears" by trying the techniques explored in chapter five, then you can use this mother to create new children. These may be: "I am capable of fighting my fear of inadequacy," "My fears will never be able to overpower me," and, "I am powerful enough to face my fear of failure."

By creating one mother, it is much easier for you to create more children and other mothers to pad up your arsenal of self-belief and empowering thoughts. And if you look into changing your existing negative beliefs at the same time, the number of moths will reduce simultaneously.

Gradually, this wing of the internal residence will change from being full of bs boxes and moths to being organised and full of power-up beliefs instead, as you navigate through yourself and your life.

By choosing to create belief systems where your positive beliefs work together, you can create a powerful network of support within yourself. These belief systems can help you grow stronger, overcome fears, and live with greater clarity and confidence.

Decide to Believe

One of the easiest ways to adopt a new belief and change an old one is to just decide. I have suggested some methods in chapter five, though I have found that my power to decide has been incredibly helpful. Affirmations don't really work for me unless I'm doing them in EMDR (Eye Movement Desensitisation and Reprocessing). Journaling helps me unpack my thoughts, but it doesn't really change them.

Whereas, when I really want to believe something, I just make a resolute decision that this is what I believe now. End of story. There's no question about it. This is my belief.

This may seem unlikely or difficult, but think about it. If you can so quickly adopt unconscious beliefs without thinking about them, why can't you do this just as easily consciously?

The trick is figuring out what's holding you back from adopting this belief. Sometimes, I've found that I'm just not willing to. I want to believe I'm powerful, but I don't. I believe the exact opposite. So, how do I change that? Have I even questioned what is holding me back from it?

Is it that I think it's unreasonable or unrealistic? Am I basing my willingness to believe something based on what others think? Maybe. If so, then do I want to keep letting that get in my way of empowering myself? Absolutely not.

I truly believe that if you are wanting to adopt a belief, have identified the blocks to it, and removed them or disregarded them, then you should be able to decide to adopt it—and it happens. If it doesn't happen for you, then maybe you don't believe you have the power to do this, and that power belief is one you need to consciously instill first. Or maybe you have other things blocking you, other bs boxes that need opening.

You might find this difficult. Just try it, though. Maybe try it with something meaningless like believing rain is comforting, not depressing. See if you can just decide to believe this and it happens.

Or maybe try it with creating a mother belief. However, I have found that in order to keep my mother belief alive, especially with all of my moths and rats, I must keep consciously reinforcing it. Every time I start questioning,

I shut down those thoughts, and trust that mother belief and power it up.

You will be challenged in your positive beliefs, and sometimes you will feel exhausted by this. Sometimes, you want to feel down for a few days because it's taking so much energy out of you to keep fighting for your positivity. That's okay. We're all allowed a couple of days. It can be a nice rest sometimes. But don't stay in it. Let it show you the contrast of living in self-belief versus negativity. Let it give you more evidence, supporting your choice to change your internal environment to positive because it feels so much better.

Yes, you have to thoroughly earn it. Aren't the most worthwhile things hard earned, though? If you want to change your beliefs to fear fighting instead of fear feeding, you can absolutely decide to do that.

What I don't suggest is faking it till you make it. I don't agree with anything that compromises your authenticity. If you're struggling, own it. Search for your solutions and try them until they're resolved. Don't try to pretend your internal challenges don't exist. That won't solve them. Creativity, willpower, and resourcefulness will. Empowering beliefs will.

Taking ownership of your beliefs and shaping them to be what you want them to be can be an incredible tool you can add to your tool box, helping you experience life better, especially in your endeavour of facing and fighting fear.

To summarise this chapter:

⚜ Beliefs are deeply ingrained convictions.

⚜ They can be personal, interpersonal, and impersonal.

⚜ Unconscious beliefs are those you carry without awareness or deliberate choice.

⚜ Conscious beliefs are those you've intentionally chosen to adopt.

⚜ Moths are negative beliefs that hinder and harm you, your growth and potential, and your goals.

⚜ Positive beliefs are helpful, nurturing, and supportive and have the power to reinforce each other.

⚜ Mothers are general conscious positive beliefs.

⚜ Children are situational conscious positive beliefs.

⚜ You can simply decide to believe something if you want to.

Call to Action: Try to identify and list the moths you have struggled with the most, then try to change them by either making the decision to believe the opposite or using the processes from chapter five.

Chapter Nine

Power

P ower is another wing of your internal residence. It differs from the beliefs wing, however, in that some rooms are full of bs boxes and some, or many, are completely empty. They are waiting on you to earn your power to fill them.

We are exploring power because a belief of powerlessness is often what causes the freeze response, and the belief of being able to run is what activates the run response. Alternatively, cultivating conscious beliefs of the power to face and fight our fears will then activate those responses for us.

Your powers, or rather your internal powers (as we'll explore through this chapter), have a huge influence on what you do because they determine what you believe you

are capable of doing. The more powers you believe you have, the more actions you take.

There is a distinction between the types of power, though. Like the superpowers imagined in books and movies, power comes in many forms—far more than most people realise. Sadly, the spotlight has often been on their darker side, glorifying a negative version of power. It's been represented as greed driven. However, there is another side to the story—a positive, constructive form of power that you can earn for yourself. This is not greed driven; rather, it enables internal growth and assists your pursuit of your goals, such as fighting your rats and black cats.

External Power

The media often portrays power as something gained by holding authority over others, but that portrayal places more value on gaining power for yourself than on using it to benefit others.

It also perpetuates the beliefs that power can only be gained by taking it away from others, and power equals control. This representation convinces people that external achievements and authority are the only forms of growth and expansion worth pursuing. It leads us to desire external expansion alone, without changing anything within ourselves.

What many fail to realise is that those fixated on accumulating external power become controlled by their

pursuit of it. I'm not shaming those who are in pursuit of external power; rather, I'm trying to show you that it's not the only form of power to exist. And in my opinion, it's not the one we benefit the most from earning. For those willing to take on the heavy responsibility required, it can be a great avenue for maturity. However, that's not the case for many.

Allow me to explain. External power can consume those who see it as their only value. They are deceived into thinking they are fulfilled by their perceived expansion, when in reality, they have only changed superficially.

Those who relish the feeling of being socially above others, who take pleasure in treating those in service to them as inferior, unknowingly pay a high price for the power they crave. It's not just a simple exchange—it is a sacrifice of themselves. The more they grasp and hoard, the more of themselves they lose.

Their most cherished possession now holds them captive.

They live in constant fear of losing their power. Every thought, every action, is driven by this fear and their need to avoid facing the danger, because it is something that can be lost.

I am presenting external power in such a negative way to warn you that in your sole pursuit of it, you can lose yourself. This is different to internal power, which is where you become more of your true self.

Internal Power

External power is easily understood in the context of the employer-employee relationship. An employer takes responsibility for providing financial stability to their employees in exchange for their time and skills. In doing so, they hold the power to dictate how that time is spent. The employee, in turn, has little say in how that time is used.

On the other hand, self-employed people hold complete control over their time. They take on risks and responsibilities, but no one has the power to dictate how they spend their hours. In this regard, no one holds power over them. This is a good example of internal power— power to control your use of time.

The ability to take full responsibility for yourself and have complete self-control is one of the most valuable forms of power you can cultivate.

Control over yourself begins by addressing everything you feel out of control with, internally—namely, all of the rats and black cats. The killer comfort blankets and bs boxes. The moths. This is done by challenging and dismantling beliefs that do not serve you, as well as acknowledging and healing from past traumas and pains that still haunt you.

By eliminating these internal blocks, you gain the ability to consciously maintain control over your state of being. You aren't in a constant battle for dominance with

the rats and their friends anymore. Instead, you take back the reins.

You become solely responsible for your actions and emotions. Yes, this is a difficult endeavour to achieve, and there is the possibility that you never have complete control over your internal self. The pursuit of it is what matters, though. Moving towards self-actualisation gives you something positive and rewarding to dedicate your life to.

But control is just one form of internal power. It is not the only type of power that exists. There are many others waiting to be discovered and harnessed by you.

There is the power to change and create new beliefs, something we've explored thoroughly through the book, as it may be your greatest ally in your fear-facing and fighting journey. The power of honesty—your ability to speak the truth without fear or hesitation. The power to process your emotions—understanding and managing them quickly, as well as the power of conscious decision-making.

The reason I love the concept of internal powers is that they level you up in every area of your life, not just one. External powers are usually just one.

Your journey of life can become a quest to uncover and earn all of these inner powers—if you decide you want to earn them. Ultimately, you choose whether you want to tap into your full potential and become the strongest and happiest version of yourself. Yes, doing so means conquering your fears—and we'll get back to that soon. But we have a little more to discuss when it comes to power, starting with its relationship to responsibility.

The Relationship between Responsibility and Power

Power isn't handed to you—it's something you earn through the weight of responsibility.

The more responsibility you take for yourself, the more power you have over your own life. Every choice, every action—all builds towards mastering yourself. This doesn't work the same way when it comes to external power. The power you gain from taking responsibility for others is tiny compared to what you could achieve by owning every part of your own life.

It's like comparing a flicker of a match to a roaring wildfire.

When you take even a little responsibility for yourself, you start regaining some control. But when you fully own it—every decision, every consequence—you tap into an endless source of power within you.

And the best part? This kind of power isn't rigid or limited. It grows, shifts, and adapts to what life throws at you. It's yours to use as you need.

Now, let's talk about taking responsibility for others. It might feel like you're stepping into a position of power, but the truth is, the weight of looking after someone else far outweighs any personal power you gain. When you're responsible for others, their needs and well-being come first. Your growth and freedom take a back seat.

External power—the kind that comes from authority over others—can be a heavy burden that doesn't give back as much as it takes. If you neglect your responsibilities or abuse that power, it will be taken away.

Real power isn't about controlling others—it's about mastering yourself. That's where the magic happens. The power you gain from taking responsibility for yourself is different. No one can take it from you. It's yours. It's untouchable.

This is why self-responsibility matters so much. You become powerful from it. But society doesn't always teach us that. We're told that taking on other people's burdens is more noble—that it's more important. It's helping them.

Is it? Or are we just holding them back, robbing them of the chance to grow and figure things out for themselves? And are we robbing ourselves of our own freedom or our ability to pursue our own personal responsibility?

I'm not saying you should never help someone, but sometimes we turn into pseudo-parents for people who don't need it, just because it makes us feel good or we believe we should or are obliged to. It can give us a false sense of purpose.

But I believe my responsibility to myself comes before any responsibility to anyone else. The reason for this is not lazy or selfish. Rather, I believe it is better for me to learn how to solve my problems myself, rather than constantly asking others to join and support me on my journey when they all have their own problems to deal with.

We all have a limited capacity. You can't do everything for everyone—and yourself. Therefore, I believe it's more selfless to focus on targeting my capacity to myself and fulfilling my responsibilities, so I am not asking anyone else to do it for me. Yes, I get challenged and want help sometimes. But the truth is that whenever I have asked for support in the past, I haven't wanted advice.

I've wanted someone to listen to my struggle and say something like this in return: "I know you'll figure it out," "I trust you to solve your problems," "I believe in your ability to fix this."

All I needed was a reminder of my power to solve my problems, when I was struggling to remind myself. And because this is what I need, I've come to an agreement with my family. Whenever I am struggling, that's the only thing they say to me. It immediately perks me up, and I'm on my way to doing just that.

One important distinction here is that the statement, "You'll figure this out," is said with genuine belief and compassion. It's said with true confidence. It's not said out of disregard or laziness. It's not rejecting offering help; rather, recognising a reminder of power is the help needed.

I'm not saying you should never ask for or give help. I'm also not a parent, so I don't know what the experience would be to navigate this as one. I am saying, however, that most of the time, the help we need is just a reminder of our power and capability to do the thing we're struggling with. It's not that we don't have the power to do it; we've just temporarily forgotten.

And I know there are different situations for everything, and sometimes you really do need help, especially physically. Again, since I'm not a parent, I don't know how it would feel to say this to your child.

I'm not suggesting that you can solve every single problem alone. But I believe you should give it an honest try first. You never know what new powers you may earn from it.

Belief of Power

So, bringing it back to fear, write down lists answering the following questions: What are your beliefs about your powers and abilities when faced with the strand of fear and amplified danger you've chosen to face? What do you think you can or can't do? Which beliefs of power influenced the beliefs of consequence that you identified in chapter seven?

Let me walk you through an example here. Referring back to the fear-of-disappointment-from-parents example used in chapter seven, I have listed below some of the statements and linked them to potential power beliefs.

"Next, I believe my parents won't listen to my reasoning for changing my job and will kick me out of their home instead because I don't believe I have the power to calm them down and convince them to give me a chance to explain. I also don't believe I have the ability to explain myself to them in the way that they need to understand me."

"Next, I believe that they'll walk me to the door and disown me as their child because I don't have the power to show them how much I love them and remind them of how much they love me. I believe I don't have the ability to convince them against their decision because our love is more important than anything to me."

When facing your beliefs of power, you're uncovering the deeper truth about your self-perception. You may have a subconscious belief that you're more powerless than you really are. Believing that you don't have the power to do the things you want to do is disheartening. But just because you believe you're powerless or limited in power doesn't make it true.

You're not powerless; you aren't meant to be powerless.

No one is born to lead a powerless life.

A question lies within you on why you believe that you are powerless. Bring that belief out of your subconscious and study it consciously. Only then can you understand it and begin to change it. What is the origin? Who or what influenced it?

It could be as simple as remembering someone telling you that you'll never be capable of being a great chef and you accepted this as true, or maybe the first ever meal you lovingly made for your friends was rudely rejected and insulted. You might find the reasons for your belief in powerlessness are similar or connected to those for your beliefs of consequence, such as believing you don't have the ability to be a great chef means that for your fear of

inadequacy, you believe the consequence is being publicly humiliated for your dish.

Or, the reasons for your belief may be entirely different. Regardless, confronting these reasons is crucial because it provides the insight needed for you to move forwards. Understanding why you hold certain beliefs allows you to evaluate their validity and decide if you want to keep them.

If you don't know the origins, you may struggle to change the beliefs because you don't know what created them in the first place.

Once you know them, you can decide how you want to react. You can reject what the memory taught you instead of accepting it. You can take a different interpretation from the experience than the one you initially had. You're not obligated to keep holding on to a disempowering subconscious belief.

Powering Up

As explored throughout the book, you can change your beliefs, if you want to. By doing so, you can consciously choose to develop the internal powers needed to achieve your goals.

Review the list of powers you believe you do and don't have, and now draft a new list. For this strand of fear, what powers would you love to have in your arsenal to use in the face of it? What abilities would you like to possess effortlessly? How does your true self want to react?

Picture it in your mind. Envision the sequence of events and consider what you would do differently if you had those new abilities. Or, maybe you want to write it all down. Write the story of what would happen if you believed everything you want to believe. How easily would the fear and amplified danger vanish? Savour this. Bask in the magnificence of your new power.

Take your time and write the story you want to live. Equip yourself with a deep understanding of your abilities. Give yourself a genuine chance to harness the powers you need to conquer your fear and transform into someone completely different from who you've been up until now. Someone powerful.

Giving yourself the chance to see who you could become if you believed you owned your internal powers is one of the kindest things you can do for yourself. It will also encourage you to consciously change your beliefs. At the end of the day, why would you want to keep living in a painful and powerless belief system when you've vividly imagined and deeply felt how beautiful it would be to live with a powerful one instead?

Then, after you've connected with the internal powers you'd like, you have two options to earn them. You can consciously change and create new power beliefs using the techniques from chapters five and eight and then start living from this place and using these powers. So you earn the powers by creating the beliefs.

Or, you can earn the power by using it first and letting the evidence that you were able to do that thing naturally create the associated belief.

Allow me to demonstrate. Say you want to earn the power of honesty but are afraid of the reactions. You want to become someone who communicates your truth in a way that the other person receives and accepts it respectfully.

The first method to earn this is to consciously create a mother belief of "I have the power to communicate my thoughtful truth to people with respect." Then, you can either create a child belief like "I have the power to tell [this person] [this thing], and their response does not pose a danger to me." With these beliefs backing you, you use this power and say what you need to.

Or, the second method to earn this power is to go directly to the person, fears and all, and say what you need to say with respect. After you've used the power, you have evidence that you do actually have this capability, and a belief is naturally formed.

Earning this power helps you to earn the others, as you've got evidence of your ability—your power—to do this. You also know what method worked for you, so you can emulate it, try the other method, or create a new one for yourself to see what else works.

What happens if these methods don't work, and you don't earn the new power? Try again. Try a different method. Keep trying. Don't give up. You just need to work harder and smarter to earn them for yourself.

In doing this, you find and create yourself—your *real* self—and you experience life the way you want to. What you don't do is live your life afraid of things that you have amplified the threat or severity of—things that likely won't happen, or pains that you could easily or moderately experience and grow from instead. You won't be sabotaging yourself out of believing you're powerless before your fears.

You will live in power instead. Not in unconscious fear. As everyone should.

To summarise chapter nine:

- There are many forms of power.

- The media portrays external power to control others to be the main one.

- Internal power, however, takes many forms.

- The relationship between power and responsibility differs based on whether it's internal or external.

- Looking at your beliefs of power and the reasons behind them will help you to consciously change and cultivate them.

- Giving yourself the chance to claim the internal powers you want and need is one of the kindest things you can do for yourself.

You can earn internal powers by either creating a mother belief of them and then using the power or using the power through fear, and the belief is formed naturally from the evidence you've gained.

Call to Action: What are your thoughts on your internal powers? Do you believe you have any? Do you believe you can have more? If you don't, take a moment to try to challenge and change this belief.

Chapter Ten

Needs

Finally, we will now explore needs, which are also their own wing of your internal residence. Differing from beliefs and powers, this wing is so full of towers of bs boxes you can't even walk around the room. There is so much we don't know about our internal needs. For this book, we will focus on how they relate to our fears.

As much as you may resist acknowledging it, as a human being, you have a wide array of needs—both numerous and varied. Yes, you're well aware of your physical necessities, such as food, water, and sleep. You shape your daily routine around these needs, understanding their importance. There are times when you neglect them, and in doing so, you suffer. When you

go without eating or sleeping, the discomfort gnaws at you until the need is met.

Some might view these as vulnerabilities. It can be frustrating to feel the sharp pangs of hunger or the relentless ache of sleep deprivation. But these needs also regulate you. They nourish and sustain you, keeping you grounded and alive.

While your physical needs are undeniable, you also have internal needs that crave attention. These are often overlooked or misunderstood, leading to silent suffering when even one goes unmet. These needs demand the same respect and prioritisation as physical ones.

I can't definitively list all your internal needs, as I assume they are deeply personal and unique to each person. I do believe there is a universal set of internal needs shared by all humans, such as parental love, acceptance, and appreciation of vulnerability—an interesting topic worth a thorough exploration, though one for a future book. I have noticed a lot of our internal needs are interpersonal, in that they exist in connection with other people. However, I won't be able to cover every topic related to needs in depth here, such as every way to meet them, as that really is a journey in itself.

Hungry Necessities

To grasp the impact of unmet needs, let's compare them to something familiar—hunger. Imagine your unmet internal

need (your need for positive social connection, for example, or your need to express emotion) as a ravenous, even starving, stomach. It desperately needs food. Urgently. The longer it goes unfed, the more intense the pain becomes.

Right now, the pain is so extreme it feels like your stomach might devour itself and your ribs will cave in. It's absolutely unbearable. Plus, the malnutrition has left you faint and lightheaded. Your thoughts are scattered, your temper is short, and you just need some food.

This is exactly what your neglected internal needs are doing to you. The biggest difference is what you fear. With physical needs, you don't fear your stomach or the food. You do fear deprivation of the need, however—which is, not getting the food you need and staying in starvation. That pain of deprivation is real and is something you need to avoid in order to survive.

Internally there are two forms of fear I have seen created. There is the fear of deprivation of a need, like physical needs. I *do not* believe this to be a rat (unconscious permanent internal fear) and black cat (amplified danger) situation. This is a matter of your internal survival, and meeting this need is how you do that. This can actually be quite a helpful fear, as it motivates you to find solutions to avoid the chance of your needs being deprived. They promote internal resourcefulness.

This is limited, however, when you believe there is only one possible way for your need to be met and that happens to be something unhealthy and unsustainable. I don't believe there are many situations where there is

only one possible way to meet a need. Most of the time, you just need to put effort into finding other sustainable and healthy sources.

The second form of fear is fear of the need itself. This is something I *do* believe to be a rat and black cat situation. Your needs, physical or internal, are not a danger to you. Rather, their unfulfillment is the cause of your pain; that is the danger. The need in itself is not, meaning fearing it is not necessary.

Belief of Need

So, for the strand of fear you're focussing on, can you identify if one of your internal needs is linked to it? Is the thing you're afraid of actually a need that you believe is a danger to you? If it is, and you clearly identify this, then you'll be able to change your relationship with it entirely.

Alternatively, are you afraid of your need not being met anymore? Maybe you're not afraid of the need itself, but of the pain you'd experience from it not being satisfied. This is a justified fear, and understanding it will help you understand the need, how you've been fulfilling it, and open you to finding alternative sources for it, if necessary.

Your beliefs about your needs are dictating how you respond to them. The beliefs determine whether you view the needs in a positive or negative light and how effectively you're willing and able to meet them.

If you have moths (negative beliefs) about your internal needs, seeing them as dangerous and thus something to fear and avoid, you won't be choosing to get to know them better. Instead, you'll avoid them and create more distance, which makes you more depleted and deprived—in more pain.

On the other hand, if you're afraid of your need not being met, you're going to panic and do anything you can to ensure that doesn't happen. Even if your need has been satisfied with unhealthy methods, such as fulfilling your need for friend love with someone who's manipulative and emotionally abusive. You know you don't feel good after spending time with them, but your need is being met and so you're content to continue that relationship. You may even believe that this friend is the *only* source to meet your need. This is not sustainable and is damaging you in its own way. It's also not true. Therefore, shifting your focus to finding a better way, such as changing those beliefs and finding a better friend, would be a way to resolve the situation.

So, what do you believe about your needs, and do you know how you've been responding to them?

Intimacy

Let's work through an example of the rat and black cat situation, i.e., fearing the need itself. When it comes to the running response, many people don't know what they're

running from, why they're running, or even when their flight began (explored in chapter six). One particularly common fear is the fear of intimacy—a complex and often misunderstood experience. This fear usually triggers a flight response, causing people to turn away, avoid connection, and retreat into solitude. They do this because they believe intimacy poses a threat to their well-being.

The idea of letting someone in and exposing their vulnerabilities feels like standing on the edge of a cliff, staring into the unknown depths below.

Intimacy can be built in any relationship, though a romantic connection may provide the most ideal environment to nurture it. To me, intimacy feels like being wrapped in a warm, welcoming hug. It's the act of opening yourself completely to someone who embraces you with open arms. Intimacy is the bond formed through the ongoing practice of that warm, welcoming hug. This connection has a profound ability to lift you above the chaos and struggles of daily life. It melts away your worries and dissolves your stress, leaving behind a sense of calm and lightness. Intimacy, like a rare and precious gem, is a gift that deserves reverence and gratitude.

Yet, this treasure is not easily attained. It requires effort, vulnerability, integrity, and courage. To truly experience intimacy, you must take a leap of faith, exposing your raw, unguarded self. You risk judgement and rejection—of your flaws, your truths, and every part of who you are— in the hope of being met with warmth, appreciation, and unconditional acceptance.

This brave act is rewarded with deep love and acceptance without conditions or reservations—something we all long for.

In the grand tapestry of human experience, intimacy is a need.

Running from Intimacy

How do people run from this need they are afraid of? Let me begin by stating an undeniable truth: You cannot actually outrun your needs. It's simply impossible. You might attempt to numb the pain of unmet needs—through distractions, delusions, or even convincing yourself that those needs are unimportant. But none of that changes the fact that your needs remain. That said, there are three primary ways I have seen people run from their fear of intimacy, all with the same objective: avoiding forming close, meaningful connections with others.

The first form of running from intimacy is avoiding romantic relationships altogether. This means actively choosing to steer clear of creating any kind of intimate bond with another person. In trying to protect yourself from the pain you believe intimacy will bring, you live in a different kind of pain—the pain of intimacy deprivation. You deprive yourself of connection, growth, and the chance to heal the fear you're carrying. In the end, your efforts to avoid pain only keep you trapped in it.

The second form of running is engaging only in short-term, casual, or temporary relationships. This method is

based on the belief that by skimming the surface, you're not missing out completely. Diving deeper into a meaningful relationship feels too risky, so this way you get the good stuff without the bad, right? But with this approach, you choose partners who won't challenge your fears or push you towards growth. You gravitate towards relationships that feel "safe" because they lack the depth required to confront your fear of intimacy. You avoid the risk of true connection by staying in shallow waters.

The final form of running is settling into a long-term relationship that feels safe from intimacy. This type of relationship is built on surface-level interactions, like gossip or mundane everyday issues, rather than meaningful connection. It's a relationship of stagnant comfort, where both partners are too afraid to engage with the vulnerability and transformation intimacy demands, leaving both people stuck in a space of unfulfilled potential.

The damage caused by running from intimacy is profound. You rob yourself of every opportunity to experience the richness and fulfillment that intimacy can bring. You might allow yourself just enough intimacy to fulfill a want, to stave off the hunger for deeper connection—a breadcrumb to survive on. But in doing so, you deprive yourself of the nourishment your deepest needs crave. You're left depleted, and in pain.

Is that really the experience you want to have in life?

Of course not. So why let fear hold you back? Why keep running?

Finding Your Needs

You run because you believe your internal needs are a danger to you. However, as relentless as they may be, your needs are *not* dangerous. What truly causes your distress is a lack of awareness about them and the decision to fear those needs instead of embracing them. This mindset keeps you stuck in a cycle of suffering, where your needs remain either starved or poorly fulfilled.

What is the solution to this? Well, you have the ability and responsibility to create a nurturing environment within yourself, one that welcomes and supports the fulfillment of your needs. You have the power to decide how *all* your needs will be met—every single one of them. However, you need to find them and learn about them first.

Just like some people dedicate hours to learning about their physical nutrition, the same kind of effort is essential for understanding your *internal* nutrition. To start, dig into your cravings. What are you emotionally yearning for? What experiences do you long for? What have you felt deprived of in your life? Try to see things from a different perspective.

Let me walk you through an example. I believe that love, as an experience and energy source, has many forms. And they are mostly, if not all, internal needs. Socially, our attention is mostly drawn to self and romantic love. If you really break it down, though, there are many forms of it. We'll focus on family love as an example here. You

could view it as a general need, or you could break it down into its individual categories based on relationships—predominantly parental love and sibling love. Even those break down into maternal and paternal love, and sister and brother love.

Personally, I've identified that each one of these is an internal need. I'm very blessed, and I have an incredibly loving family dynamic with my parents and brothers. I realised, though, that sometimes when we are distanced from each other, I miss the specific form of love that person in that role provides me. And yes, there is the element of me loving that individual. However, in the alternative situation where I wasn't close with, say, my brother, I would feel the loss of that brotherly love. I know that during disagreements, many people feel the big loss of love from that role in their lives—or maybe they've never experienced it. It has its own essence that I need to be fed to meet my need.

If I misunderstand this need, I could see it as a sign of weakness. I could even fear it. However, if I observe it and look at what's missing, I can figure out what I need to do to fulfill it. For example, as I don't have a biological sister, I meet my need for sisterly love with my cousins and friends. These relationships satisfy my need.

The ache you feel doesn't come from the needs themselves but from misunderstanding, neglecting, and fearing them. Your needs are not the enemy—they are the essential elements that support and sustain you. You just

need to be willing to understand them and yourself in turn.

Wants vs. Needs

We need our needs—that is clear. But what you do to meet them is a whole other story. You have the power to decide *whether* you'll consciously address them or not. You also have the freedom to choose *how* you'll try to meet them.

The way you think your needs *should* and *can* be fulfilled and the way they actually *need* to be fulfilled are often worlds apart. And, more often than not, people get it wrong. There are two big reasons for this. The first being that most people don't understand them well enough. However, that's what the section above covered.

The second reason people struggle to meet their internal needs ties directly to the first: When you don't fully understand what your true needs are, you often label them as mere wants.

From this place, you start believing your yearning to satisfy a need is just a want. And yes, of course you *want* to satisfy it, but wants are like passing shadows—temporary and fleeting—while needs are the deep, unshakable roots of an ancient tree. Every time you fulfill one of these fleeting wants, it only satisfies the need for a brief moment. But the need itself remains hungry, insatiable, and constant. It will always demand more—just as you will always need more food, always need more sleep, every day you are alive.

A need is never fully satisfied, never ending. Wants, on the other hand, are finite and short-lived.

When you try to meet your needs by chasing wants, you're not addressing the core issue.

This is why, even after satisfying a want, you might still feel unhappy. There's a lingering hunger for something more—an endless cycle of chasing the next thing, and the next, and the next. You're left wondering: *Why doesn't this make me happy? Why do I still feel miserable? Why does the suffering never end?*

Your intentions are honest, your efforts genuine, but they're misaligned with what you're truly striving for. It's like chasing a mirage—each time you think you're close, it vanishes, leaving you thirsty for real, lasting contentment.

As this pain and confusion take over, negative beliefs begin to take root. You start seeing the very thing you long for—the need left unmet—as a threat. Why? Because your mind begins associating the unmet need with the suffering it's causing. It's only natural to question: *How could something that causes so much pain not be a threat?*

That is how we end up fearing intimacy, change, and a myriad of other things that are actually good for us.

Fulfilling a Need

After finding and understanding your need, how do you consciously meet it? And how do you stop fearing it? Well, there are many different options. The most powerful course

of action I can advise is creating a conscious permanent internal fear for yourself. They are my secret weapon when something is non-negotiable for me.

You can replace your fear of the need with the fear of deprivation of it instead. Or rather, you can overpower the unconscious fear with a conscious fear. This is the thing that drives my whole personal journey with facing and fighting my fears and learning about how to meet my internal needs. I'm consciously afraid of the alternative.

How do you do this? The first step is emotionally connecting with the deprivation danger and seeing it for what it is—a real threat to your internal well-being and survival. Connect with the pain of that deprivation you've already experienced and may be experiencing now. Truly believe it is something you want to avoid.

And then, let this conscious fear give you the energy and drive your need to be resourceful and creative with your solutions. Every need is unique, and each person will meet it in their own ways. Take the need of parental love. There is such a wide spectrum in terms of the degrees of which this is met by people. For some, it is being healthily met by their biological parents; for others, it is by their adopted parents; for others, it's being met by older family friends. On the other end of the scale, it's not being met at all, reasons varying.

Depending on your situation, you can start finding a solution. I'm not saying your need will always be met in the way your heart desires the most, such as if your parents have unfortunately passed away. You can find *some* way to

feed your need, though. It's not about trying to replace that person but choosing to not live in internal need deprivation for the rest of your life.

Say you want to meet this need with your older family friends. You don't need to tell them that you'd like them to provide you with parental love, but you can open yourself to receiving it from them if that's something they're already sharing. Let that experience be a conscious source of nourishment for you.

Or maybe you would like to open up to them and tell them that parental love is something you are feeling deeply deprived of, and you would greatly appreciate it if you could form a closer relationship with them in this way. And depending on their answer, hoping they say yes, you've created a conscious source of nourishment. If they say no, you can try something else.

Resourcefulness and creativity is the key here. A conscious fear of deprivation drives those two things without needing to force yourself to keep moving forwards towards your goal. The thing that holds you back is an unconscious fear of the need itself, which is what you don't need to hold on to.

To end part four, I am hoping that the three topics explored here—beliefs, power, and needs—have shone a light on some considerations for your rats and black cats that you may not have been aware of. Consciously harnessing each one of these is incredibly empowering, and they are excellent tools to use when analysing and creating an awareness of your fears.

To conclude this chapter and part four, sometimes we don't realise how our beliefs are affecting us, or that we think we're powerless. We don't see that the thing we're afraid of is what we need the most. Facing your fears and seeing these things gives you the chance to respond to them differently and take ownership of them.

To summarise chapter ten:

A deprivation of internal needs affects us in the same ways as physical ones.

Sometimes we fear the deprivation of our needs, which can be a helpful fear in our journey to meet them.

However, sometimes, we fear our internal needs.

These fears are rats and black cats. They are unconscious permanent internal fears sabotaging us as they deprive us of the internal nourishment we need.

We change this situation by finding our internal needs, understanding them, and then consciously meeting them.

Creating a conscious permanent internal fear of the deprivation of our need is the most powerful thing we can do to stop fearing the need itself, as it fuels our resourcefulness and creativity to meet it.

Call to Action: Can you identify one internal need you are afraid to be deprived of and one need you are afraid of? Are you willing to overpower the second one with a conscious deprivation fear?

PART FIVE

A Conscious
Response

Chapter Eleven

Principles To Live By

P art three was an exploration of the way you have most likely been responding to your rats and black cats thus far, and part four was an exploration of three topics that will have likely greatly influenced why you've been freezing and running.

Part five will be an exploration of three techniques you can use to remove yourself from an instinctive fear response to a conscious response of facing or fighting your fear instead.

Sometimes, we are so deep in the experience of being afraid that it is difficult to remove ourselves from it long enough to start thinking clearly and questioning our rats (unconscious permanent internal fears), black cats (amplified dangers), and moths (negative beliefs).

Chapter eleven will explore responding to fear out of beliefs and principles of obligation, and changing that with conscious life principles. Chapter twelve will explore conscious anger as a tool to break free from being frozen in fear, and finally, chapter thirteen will explore conscious character traits.

Let's begin.

What is a principle of life? I define it as a belief I consciously use to shape my decisions, actions, and reactions to optimise my experience of life. To simplify this, it's a belief that you live by. Something that guides your way through life, through all successes and challenges.

The difference between a principle and belief is that a principle is an especially important belief you have chosen to navigate your life by. An example is, "I will live my life protecting my peace and happiness at all costs." Other beliefs, such as, "I prefer to write with gel pens over other pens," aren't exactly as important or what you might use to guide all major and minor life decisions.

Principles of life can be an excellent ally in your fight against fear, especially if you've consciously chosen and resolutely planted them. They can also be the reason why you've been responding to your rats and black cats in a helpless way thus far.

Now, do you know what your life principles are? Have you chosen any? There is a chance you haven't, as it's something that seems to be subtly woven into our experience of life, yet we haven't solidified it into a resolute principle. Principles like "everything happens for a reason"

are very commonly held these days, and are great. They just don't seem to be consciously chosen as a principle of life.

Instead, I think people are living by unconscious principles of life. The ones I have seen most commonly held are principles of obligation. These are the beliefs that your life should be navigated and lived filling your obligations to other people. And in this, you take action and respond to situations, like your fears, based on what others have taught you that you should do, not what you want to believe and do.

Obligations

Obligations encompass all your "shoulds"—everything you believe you should do or should be.

Are you believing something because you believe you should, rather than because you genuinely want to?

Are you afraid of something simply because you believe you should be afraid of it, not because you want or need to be afraid of it?

Are you responding to fear the way you believe you should, rather than how you want and need to?

Genuinely consider if you are living by principles of obligation, rather than principles of life you have consciously chosen to live by. This is important because, if you are, you are living life and responding to fears out

of a sense of duty and obligation, not out of consciousness and free will.

These principles of obligation may have been imposed upon you, so you've been taught to believe you have to live your life out of duty and instruction by those certain people. You were led to believe your obligation to them trumps all your free will. Elders can do this to children sometimes. And if you were taught to fear your elders, then the belief you need to fear them out of obligation will be ingrained within you. It will be embedded so deeply that it becomes a principle in general, that your life is meant to be lived based on what others are telling you that you should do.

Another reason might be that you've unknowingly seen someone else do something or react to something in a certain way, and you feel obligated to do the same. You may even live by a principle of obligation determined by how others live, rather than how others are telling you to live.

For example, you may believe you need to shrink in the face of your fears just because you've seen someone whom you trust and respect do the same. Maybe you think you should be afraid of facing your fears because everyone around you is. Maybe your friends all have anxiety about their exams, so you believe you must have a fear of failure as well. After all, how could you possibly have self-confidence in your efforts and an assurance that failure is a pain you will survive?

So, bringing it back to your strand of fear, look through your timeline from the beliefs of consequence (chapter

seven) and your beliefs of power (chapter nine) and check whether the reason for any of those beliefs is simply that you think you should believe it, nothing else. If the only reason you believe or do things is because you believe that you should believe and do them, because you believe you are obligated to, then you didn't exactly choose them, did you?

I don't want you to be living out of a sense of permanent self-sacrificing imposed duty. I particularly don't want you to be doing this because you have been led to believe that this makes you a good person, and this is the only way you can be one. Oftentimes, another's moral compass is imposed upon you before you're given the chance to set it for yourself, and so the obligations imposed are set by their moral compasses, not yours. You may believe their moral compass is yours. How can you know that, though, without setting it for yourself?

This is why I encourage you to question your obligations and determine whether you want to keep them or not. Not all obligatory beliefs are helpful, well informed, or reasonable. In fact, most are probably the opposite. By questioning them and deciding to implement conscious helpful ones instead, you can free and empower yourself.

Questioning a Principle of Obligation

How do you question a principle of obligation? Well, it's the same process as questioning the other beliefs we've

explored through the book thus far. You identify the obligation, the reason for it, and then analyse both of them.

So, find an obligation, such as, "I must be respectful to everyone at all times, even when they are rude or disrespectful." Identify where it came from, likely your parents in this situation. And then question: Is this something you logically think is a good idea? Is it something you want to do without the guilt of being a good person attached to it?

The second question may be harder to answer honestly because it can be tough to take yourself out of the good-person guilt trip sometimes. I've experienced the same thing. Plus, what often happens is you develop a fear of being a bad person by not fulfilling your obligations, even when they aren't serving you, such as in the face of fear.

You have two options here: You can ask a friend—who doesn't have the same obligations as you—to help review and question yours. Or, you can consciously define your moral compass, what being a good person means to you, and then return to questioning your beliefs of obligation.

I am going to circle back to how conscious life principles can help you escape an unconscious fear response. However, I would like to take a minute to explore setting your moral compass first, as this will help you quickly disregard prior obligations that don't fit your new moral compass, and so they have no place in your current way of life.

How do you set your moral compass? Begin by detaching yourself from what you've been told it should

be and identifying what feels right to you. I do this by focussing on what I hold most dearly and centring my moral compass around protecting that.

Allow me to demonstrate. Personally, my peace, happiness, and well-being are the most important things in my life, as well as my conscious character traits (CCTs), which we'll explore in chapter thirteen. I will protect them at all costs, because, the truth is, I didn't always have them. They are the centre of my moral compass, because my right and wrong depend on what is helping, hindering, or harming me in my protection of them. Therefore, any obligations I held that sacrifice them have no place in me.

For example, I used to live by the obligation that to be a good person, I have to be a nice person. To everyone. Even people who have hurt me, are trying to hurt me, and will continue to hurt me. In living by this obligation, I was sacrificing my peace, happiness, well-being, integrity, bravery, self-respect, and honesty. This obligation made me betray my true self and live as someone else. Therefore, after much deliberation, I concluded that if being a nice person means sacrificing any of those, then being nice is what will be sacrificed.

I'm not rude or disrespectful or trying to hurt anyone, but I don't believe I become a bad person by valuing peace and self-respect, over not insulting someone who's hurting me, whether they are deliberate or are oblivious about it. I will communicate what I need to, and I don't mind being labelled as "not a nice person" by someone who hasn't been the same to me. And, honestly, I love this part of me. I earn respect for myself every time I live by it.

So, have a genuine think about what you want your moral compass to be. This is not done in a day, of course, but you can start by focussing on fear.

Principle of Fearing Pain

When you find yourself spiraling into a deep pit of fear, you need something to snap yourself out of it. A conscious life principle can serve as an excellent tool for this.

Sometimes fears are heavy. Sometimes, they are filled with extreme pain from your past, pain you are afraid to experience again. This is what I experienced with my fear of bad health changes. So, how do you avoid repeatedly experiencing that pain?

You can snap out of the heavy fear by choosing principles to ground you through every high and low of your life. Choose things that will help you build new, strong, positive beliefs. These principles should be easy to remember and ones you truly want to live by. For example, the principle I chose to get past my fear of bad health is "there is always some goodness existing in every situation," so I don't need to be as afraid of bad health changes because there will be something to balance the pain of the situation. It won't be as bad as I fear it will be.

Try to choose something that renders your fears powerless just by thinking about it. An effective method is

adopting a specific and opposing perspective. For example, recently I realised that if pain is the thing I am afraid of, I don't need to welcome it, but I don't need to reject it either because I am used to experiencing pain.

No one goes through life without experiencing pain—physical and internal. We're used to taking and processing pain. One could even say that we're good at experiencing pain. Yes, everyone deals with their various pains differently, including drugs, alcohol, and escapism, while others try to consciously process the pain without numbing it away so it transforms quicker.

No matter how we deal with it, we are all highly experienced pain takers. So why would you be afraid of something you have experienced so much already? And you survived, and eventually thrived, every time. Which means that even though we amplify the belief that this specific pain is a severe threat to our survival, it's not, because we can take it. Because we've likely taken worse in the past.

This shift in perspective strips fears of their power to affect you. It shifts your perspective of you, not the fear or danger. You move from believing you are fragile and breakable to realising you are not. In fact, you are strong and a natural healer. You don't have to become a masochist and enjoy pain, but you can realise that the pain you fear isn't going to break you.

Therefore, based on these realisations, I have recently adopted a new principle of life in the face of my fears: "I'm strong enough to take this pain for what is most

important to me." If the choice is between running away from pain and staying in fear versus fighting for what's most important to me and risking a little pain, I'll walk forwards knowing that I can take it. I don't need to be afraid of it because I can handle it. And I'm hoping this will shift your perspective as well.

I believe most of us are afraid of things because we believe that we should be afraid of them, not because we honestly think we'll be harmed by them. Not because we've assessed our ability to take the hit and stay standing. Not because we know that if we fall, we'll just get back up.

Living by fearing most, if not all, pain robs you of the knowledge of your strength. It steals your confidence to stay standing and get back up when things get tough. It makes you believe you can't.

But you can. Because you always have. Even if you struggled through all of it, even if it took longer to get back up than you would like. Even if it took a long time to heal the pain. Even if you feel weak and broken from it, not stronger. None of that matters because you still took it, healed from it, and moved forwards. Every time. And you can, and will, do it again and again in the future.

Especially in the face of your fears.

Pick Your Principles

So, arm yourself with the principles that are going to help you live life the way you want to. Pick ones that help snap

you out of the clutches of your fears. Your life principles should help you through every challenge and experience of life. They should make your life better, not worse. I can't tell you what they should be. You should take your time to develop and pick the principles you really want to live by.

I can share some of mine, however, which include: "Anything is possible," "There is always something to receive, as the Universe exists in balance," "I'm willing to take this pain for what I want," and "I can solve all of my problems."

Other examples include: "Nothing is too great a challenge for me," "There is some goodness in everyone," and "I don't have to be afraid just because the world wants me to be."

To end chapter eleven, I wish you luck in choosing yours. Mine didn't come to me in one day but were developed over the past few years from the different things I experienced. Start with developing ones to help you respond to your fears better.

To summarise chapter eleven:

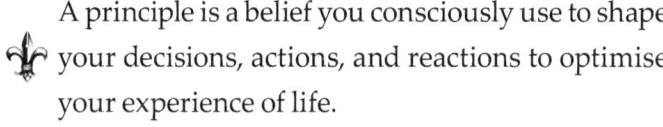 A principle is a belief you consciously use to shape your decisions, actions, and reactions to optimise your experience of life.

Principles of life can be an excellent ally in your fight against fear.

Most people live by unconscious principles of life, most commonly, principles of obligation.

An excellent way to assess your beliefs of obligation and disregard them is to consciously define your moral compass for yourself.

Most people fear a danger because they are afraid of pain—pain they believe they are obliged to fear and avoid.

If you assess your capability to take pain and how it has not broken you, but made you stronger, you realise most of the black cats you fear threaten you with pain you can handle.

Call to Action: Reflect on the moral compass you've been living by. Write down the moral beliefs and principles that come up for you, and assess each one based on its suitability to help you live the life you want. Disregard or change the beliefs and principles you don't want, and create new ones for yourself.

Chapter Twelve

Harnessed Anger

For this chapter, I'm going to propose something slightly strange and potentially provocative because I have found it to be an excellent way to remove yourself from a frozen or runaway response to your rats and black cats.

I want you to deliberately create a rage response towards your fear.

Choose to hate your fear with every fibre of your being. Let the very thought of it fill you with an incredible sense of disgust. I likened your internal fears to rats for this very reason. I want you to be disgusted by them and the reality they've created for you.

Stop feeling comfortable in the company of your rat-infested home. Trembling at the thought of them, or simply ignoring them, will never give you the power to abolish

them. You need to radically change your position and perception towards your fears.

While love and trust have often been sold as the way to overcome fears, they haven't worked for me. They, and all of their gentle companions, have never acted as a blade sharp enough to cut through my fear.

What has been strong and sharp enough is my anger. My pure disgust. These fiery emotions can cut through your fear and melt its force.

Your rats deserve nothing less than your full rage. They are insidious, ruining your peace of mind, tormenting you every second they live. These unconscious permanent internal fears have been influencing your thoughts, manipulating your actions, and steering your self-sabotaging decisions. They've been destroying your life experience. They are relentless tormentors, chaining you in pain and limitation. You should loathe their very existence.

Yet, you probably don't feel this way. That's understandable. Not many people are raised to hate their fears; instead, they are taught to blindly trust them, likely from childhood teachings such as not talking to strangers and staying away from an active flame. You survived by being aware of the potential dangers you were alerted to and treating them equally.

You can change this, and recognise that not all your fears deserve the same respect and trust. You can make a conscious choice to summon your anger the moment you feel the rats trying to hold you back again. To be clear, I am not saying you should be angry at all your fears; many of them help motivate you to do what you want to do. It's the rats—your unconscious permanent internal fears—you should be angry at.

Unconscious Anger

My suggestion to embrace anger might seem untraditional, but that's because most people see anger as a universally negative thing and have had bad experiences with it. Typically, they focus on the only type of anger they've encountered—unconscious anger.

Unconscious anger happens when you find yourself getting upset over something you didn't consciously choose to react angrily to. Maybe someone said or did something, or they failed to say or do something, and that set off a spark of frustration or fury within you. The true root of your reaction was a trigger you didn't intentionally create.

You didn't decide to have that trigger. Like your internal fears, these emotional triggers exist within you, but they were chosen by your subconscious without you knowing. You may have no idea when those triggers were created, which makes them dangerous—to both you and those around you.

What is an emotional trigger? I believe it's something held inside us that sparks an emotional reaction when an event or series of events happens. These can be consciously chosen or unconsciously held. Either way, they spark emotion, any emotion, such as sadness, happiness, or grief—not just anger.

Unconscious anger is dangerous because it rises without your conscious consent. It's like a sneaky storm brewing within. You have no idea of the scale of rage burning inside you. You erupt in this fury, losing yourself in the chaos—which can lead you to make significant, regrettable mistakes. Unconscious anger can inflict harm on yourself and others around you.

Anger is a powerhouse of emotional energy—a vortex of raw force.

But, it comes from a good place. It does. Anger is your defensive and protective reaction, a fiery guardian summoned when you believe an injustice has, is, or will happen. You feel wronged, wounded by an event, so your anger flares up in response.

When you act under the influence of unconscious anger, you're not always fully aware of which part of yourself or someone else you're protecting or which beliefs sparked the trigger. The reason why you struggle to calm down eludes you.

Why did this specific issue hit such a sensitive spot? Why did a small setback instantly spiral into frustration and stress? What makes your well of patience dry so quickly? These questions remain unanswered.

You didn't consciously choose this rage, which is why it's so incomprehensible—and so dangerous.

However, you can transform it. Alchemise it. You can begin this journey of change by permitting yourself to nurture your emotional maturity.

Systems and Triggers

We've been exploring beliefs throughout the book and how they form complex belief systems that then direct our line of thinking along a set path. With unconscious belief systems, we are led down thought path ways that we haven't chosen for ourselves. Whereas conscious belief systems are based upon path ways we have chosen, so they help us to reach the desired conclusion quicker.

I believe our emotional triggers are the second part of this puzzle. Or rather, they are the second entity existing within our belief systems. I actually believe our emotional triggers are a decision held within our belief systems.

Our belief systems exist as an incredibly complex maze. I believe all our unconscious and conscious beliefs merge to form one interconnected maze. The walls of the maze are our beliefs that link to one another. When we go down a path of thoughts, those belief walls guide us to our set destination. When we change our beliefs, the walls change, thus the path changes.

Imagine this maze exists behind the internal residence from chapter three. The maze is an extension of what is held inside the residence. So the beliefs held inside the beliefs wing are then represented in an intricate maze behind the home to show how they all connect with and affect each other.

Now, within that maze exists many emotional triggers, which are placed at the end of thought paths. For topics that are purely logical and unemotional, an emotional trigger won't exist at the end, as you've decided it's not suitable or required for that situation. It'll likely be an unemotional action instead, even if that action is to just actively forget something. Whereas, for topics that are personal, emotional, and maybe wound opening, emotional triggers are present and activate an emotional response from you.

Allow me to demonstrate. I promise this is relevant for creating a conscious response to your fears; I just need to make this point clear first. Imagine you are someone who consistently gets angry at your siblings for a specific action, say they poke you. Your beliefs have guided your thoughts to having that emotional reaction each time.

Your beliefs may be the following sequence:

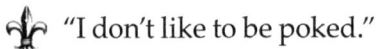 "I don't like to be poked."

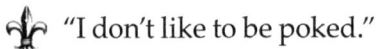 "I don't want my siblings to poke me anymore."

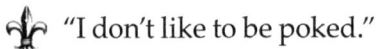 "My siblings ignore me every time I tell them to stop."

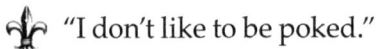 "So it's justified for me to get angry every time I am poked."

The walls of the maze are these beliefs that lead you to the destination of an emotional trigger that is, "I'm angry

every time I'm poked." And so, you have that emotional reaction.

If any of your beliefs change, then the path changes and so does your emotional trigger. Maybe you change the final belief to: "It's better to poke my siblings back than get angry." Then, you won't have the emotional response of anger triggered; you'll just take the action of poking them in return.

I understand this may seem slightly complicated as a theory, while being an oversimplification of our minds, but I'm trying to explain it in a way that is easiest to understand and not just information but something you can use to empower yourself.

The first thing you can do is walk backwards from your existing emotional triggers, back down the path of beliefs, to discover what makes you emotionally respond the way you do. If you're happy with the path and trigger, then consciously keep it. You are knowingly choosing to have a specific emotional reaction following a series of events or singular event, leading your thoughts to the specific destination of your trigger. Great.

Or, if there's something in that belief's pathway and emotional trigger destination you want to change, whether it's the beliefs themselves, the trigger, or both, then do that. Use the techniques explored in the book to change your existing beliefs. The best way I've found to change my emotional response is to change the belief immediately leading to it, like in the example above. This takes me to a different destination, an *intentional* destination, leading to a different emotion or action instead.

The second thing you can do is use this information to create conscious belief pathways and emotional triggers to motivate you to do the things you want to do. We'll discuss this in the next section. You can do this for any part of your life, of course, though focussing on fear is the topic of this book.

Consciously Created Anger

So, where does the connection lie in fear, anger, belief systems, and emotional triggers? This chapter is all about using anger as a way to swim yourself out of drowning in fear long enough to start thinking clearly and question your fears and the path or actions where they lead you. It's about pulling you from a helpless emotional state to a harnessed one instead. You can do this by creating a conscious path of belief walls that lead you to the destination of an emotional trigger of anger in response to your experience and awareness of being afraid.

Your path could take the following form:
Beliefs:

- "The rats are a danger to me."

- "I don't believe fear deserves my trust."

⚜ "I'm not going to let fear torture and sabotage me anymore."

⚜ "So fear deserves my anger instead."

Emotional trigger:

⚜ "Every time I realise I'm unhelpfully afraid, I'm angry at what it's doing to me, not afraid of the danger it's showing me."

To give you a more specific example, you could use the following:

Beliefs:

⚜ "My fear of not being good enough is lying to me."

⚜ "I don't believe what the fear is telling me."

⚜ "This fear does not have my trust."

⚜ "I'm angry that the fear is telling me I'm not good enough."

Emotional trigger:

⚜ "I'm going to get angry at the fear, not doubting myself anymore, every time I start to feel not good enough."

I don't believe anger is always a bad thing, especially when consciously created. It means something is important to you, and you don't want an injustice to occur. When you channel conscious anger towards the things blocking your growth and happiness, it's no longer just anger; it's energy.

It's your power to rip off the shackles that are holding you back.

Think of anger as your armour. It shields you from attacks—and aren't your unconscious permanent internal fears, your rats, doing just that? Attacking you from within? When you consciously swap out the cold, paralysing grip of fear for the fiery blaze of anger, you're removing fear's hold on you. You're giving yourself a chance to face it, fight it, and move past it.

So yes, I'm asking you to lean into the conscious anger you feel towards your fears. I'm asking you to do that by creating a conscious path of beliefs that lead you to a specifically created anger trigger against your fears. I want you to feel that spark of frustration every time fear creeps in, because these fears aren't helping you. They are hurting you, and you *should* feel angry towards them.

To summarise chapter twelve:

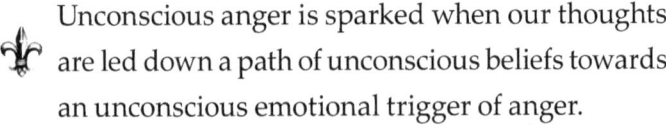 Conscious anger can be an excellent way to take yourself out of a debilitating fear response long enough to start thinking clearly.

Unconscious anger is sparked when our thoughts are led down a path of unconscious beliefs towards an unconscious emotional trigger of anger.

Our belief systems exist as an intricate maze, with our emotional triggers and actions being held in the set destinations our beliefs are leading us towards.

You can change your existing emotional reactions by changing the destination of your thoughts, even by just changing one belief in that pathway.

You can also create conscious belief pathways and emotional triggers using the techniques from the book.

Creating a pathway leading you to consciously get angry every time one of your rats is activated, instead of being afraid, is a great way to stop being afraid.

Call to Action: Can you recall a time when you responded in unconscious anger versus conscious anger? Can you make the distinctions between them, and emulate what you did with the conscious anger for your fears as well?

Chapter Thirteen

Conscious Character Traits (CCTs)

Welcome to the third topic of part five, and the final chapter of the book. Thus far in part five, we've explored how principles of life and conscious anger can be used as tools to pull you out of the experience of fear long enough to start logically thinking and questioning your fears to face them. The final tool involves choosing your conscious character traits, which we'll refer to as your CCTs.

CCTs are the qualities that you consciously decide to embody, intentionally shaping the essence of who you are. Though often socially called values, I believe the term lacks the powerful *intent* needed for you to truly connect the traits with your identity.

Consciously choosing the character traits you want to embody—the ones you want to be recognised and defined by—is maybe one of the most significant decisions you can make. This is how you design the blueprint of your identity, an intentional act of self-definition that echoes through every action and decision you make.

CCTs are the architects of your identity. They shape the essence of who you are and how you show up in the world. Examples would be integrity, kindness, and honesty. They also include courage and bravery, which we will explore in this chapter as a tool against your fears.

When you don't define your CCTs, life feels unsteady. You're untethered, floating without a foundation to guide your actions, decisions, and responses. Instead of being led by intention, you're pulled in every direction by your environment or your past, often without even realising it.

I promise I will connect CCTs with fear; however, I'd like to explore these thoroughly first. In a world that constantly pushes you to measure your value by your external achievements—career, wealth, physical form, and social status—it's easy to lose sight of what else matters. I believe your job title, bank account, body, and relationships don't define your entire being. They're just ways you interact with the world around you. They're not *you*.

Your CCTs, on the other hand, *are* the foundation of your identity. They are the traits that reflect the person you have chosen to be—not for anyone else, but for yourself. When you consciously define them, you create a foundation of inner stability. And with this stability, you

are well equipped to tackle any and all challenges sent your way, including your fears.

Choosing a Trait You Need

So, how do you choose your CCTs? Ideally, there will be a framework you use to choose them, rather than picking ones that fulfill your desire to be accepted and approved by others. The main framework guiding my choice of conscious character traits is based on my needs.

Let's begin. We explored needs, particularly internal needs, in chapter ten. Understanding our needs, our beliefs about them, and learning to fulfill them allows us to live life without being in constant, and *painful*, deprivation of them.

Something we didn't explore in that chapter was one of the ways to fulfill your needs—by embodying a CCT or multiple CCTs. Allow me to explain. One of my core needs is peace. I've mentioned this a few times throughout the book, though I haven't explained why. Peace is one of my essential needs because I become very distressed and ill without it.

This is particularly true when any form of external stress or pressure becomes a part of the equation. For example, external deadlines are extremely stressful to me, as they don't give me the time and space I need to fully think through something, especially as someone with slightly slow processing.

The existence of any deadline puts an incredible amount of stress on me. It reduces my efficiency, as I can't think clearly past my need to meet the deadline, which temporarily overpowers my need for peace. So I am consciously shaping my life and routine to accommodate my need for peace and reduce stress as much as possible.

Another thing that interrupts my peace is unnecessary and unhelpful fear. It's just there, constantly in the back of my mind, interrupting my desired train of thought by telling me to not do the things I want to do. Facing and fighting my rats is one of the ways I fulfil my need for peace.

There are a few ways I push myself forwards. First, I created a fear of the rats, as we explored in chapter one. The second is using conscious principles as a foundation of self-belief to stand on every time I lose confidence. Third, I created a conscious anger at my experience of them. The fourth is that I chose to embody the CCT of bravery.

Through my journey, I realised a multifaceted approach is required for a challenge as great as conquering my hindering and harming fears. When my fear increases, my anger comes forwards. When my anger reduces, my bravery trait moves me forwards. They interchange, motivating me to keep me going. If you would like to adopt a similar approach, I recommend choosing bravery as a conscious character trait.

Bravery

Bravery is a powerful blend of courage and determination. It's what pushes you to take the actions you need to, even when you're staring down the face of your rats and black cats. Bravery means stepping forwards, even when fear tries to pull you back. It's about refusing to retreat because your commitment to being brave outweighs your desire to stay afraid. Bravery is choosing to stand tall in the face of adversity, rather than shrinking away.

Pick bravery because you crave the chance to be tested. Let it push you to summon courage at every turn.

If you choose bravery as one of your CCTs—if you truly weave it into the very fabric of your honour and identity— it will transform the way you face your fears. Whether those fears are internal or external, bravery becomes your foundation. It's like having an unmovable wall of courage standing firmly behind you, ready to support you when fear tries to push you back.

Each time fear threatens to overwhelm you, your choice to be brave will hold you steady and push you forwards with strength and resolve.

How do you know if you're being brave? Are you brave when you do something despite being afraid? Are you brave if you do something after removing the fear of it? Are you brave if you do something you are unafraid of, though it is intimidating to others? I think it's all of these things and more.

I believe I'm being brave anytime I'm moving myself forwards despite any personally held past or present doubts and fears, as well as socially held ones. Oftentimes, what people define as being brave differs simply based on how everyone holds different fears. An action can be brave to one and not to another.

Take, for example, a job interview, which most people, especially at the beginning of their career, fear because they want the job but may doubt their value and worth. For one person, it was an incredibly brave act to step forwards and do the interview, whether they performed well or not. Turning up for the day was a huge step forwards for them. For another person, it may be bravery to respond to the interview questions with full self-belief and knowledge of their value. It may have been brave for them to have confidence in their abilities. For others, it may not have felt brave because they were not afraid; however, they were brave because this was a socially intimidating situation.

Sometimes we hold a very narrow view of what counts as bravery, usually thinking of more extreme acts, like skydiving. I believe, however, that bravery is something you embody any time fear is active in the situation, whether it's in you or someone else. Just because someone else has recognised the bravery in you before you have, doesn't mean you haven't been brave. You have; you just couldn't see it.

Maybe your friend is being bullied by another, and they are afraid of standing up for themselves. So, you protect them and communicate to the bully that their behaviour

needs to stop. You might have been nervous yourself, but you move past your fear to stop your friend being bullied. So your actions were incredibly brave in your eyes. On the other hand, you might not have been nervous, and so you did not believe you were being brave. However, your actions were still incredibly brave to your friend. They saw that in you, and so it was real.

You likely already are a brave person. You probably just don't see all of the ways you are yet. You also probably haven't claimed it as a conscious character trait. If you do choose it to be a CCT, it can be an incredible ally in your challenge with fear, because every time your fears try to hold you back from doing something you want to do, you will remember your commitment to being a brave person.

Earning Self-Respect

After you have chosen your CCTs, how do you nurture and embody them? I've embodied an "earn to keep" philosophy with my CCTs, by attaching them to my self-respect. I created a mother belief (a general conscious positive belief) that I earn respect for myself by living according to my conscious character traits.

I find earning my self-respect to be a fascinating idea, because it's not something you hear about often. Society constantly tells you to earn the respect of others, but rarely are you taught the importance of earning it for yourself—and how to do that.

So, how do you earn your own respect? Well, think about how someone else earns yours. Usually, it's because they've done something you find admirable. They've shown a quality you value, something you strive to embody in yourself, such as bravery or kindness. It's the connection of the trait you hold in high regard and their action demonstrating it.

I prefer not to value people solely for their external achievements, like their wealth or status. Instead, I give everyone the opportunity to earn my respect through their actions and behaviour. That's the same way I'm earning to keep my own—through the traits I choose to embody and the way I show up in the world.

Respect should ultimately be earned—and just as easily lost—based on someone's actions. No one should be exempt.

Earning your self-respect works the same way—it's something you consciously build through your actions. You can make this easier for yourself by setting a clear framework of CCTs, enabling you to quickly identify whether you're about to do something that is going to earn you more respect for yourself or lose it.

Let's continue with the example of bravery. I believe that I earn respect for myself every single time I do something that was either challenging for me because I was doing it despite my doubts and fears or I receive recognition from someone else for doing something that was brave. In the first instance, there were times I moved forwards with something I'm afraid of simply for two reasons: one, I really

want to move forwards with this, and two, if I don't do it, I will forever remember that I was a coward in this situation, and I will regret it.

I will be ashamed because I didn't do the thing I knew would make me proud of myself. Now look, I know how hard it can be to face and fight your fears. I know how challenging it can be to have courage. Especially, when you don't want that thing enough to be brave.

Here's an example. When I was seventeen years old, studying in Sixth Form, I applied for different legal work experiences before I applied to university. Looking around, I found two opportunities in big corporate law firms. For the first one, I didn't apply. I got intimidated, didn't believe I was good enough to even fill out the application, and backed away. For the second, I was still intimidated, but I applied because I really wanted this work experience. I wanted to apply for a job with them later, so I wanted to get my foot in the door.

The difference between my behaviour, what affected my decision to be brave or not, was how much I wanted the thing before me. With the first application, I wanted it, but I didn't want it enough to be brave. With the second, I was willing because I wanted it too much to pass up. I valued it enough to step forwards.

I'm not saying you have to be brave in every single situation of your life to earn the trait and respect of bravery. You can, if you want to. However, I'm focussing my energy and efforts on the things that matter the most to me. The things that are worth being brave for, such as my needs.

Because if they are what matters, then bravery is a no-brainer. It is simply what you must be to move forwards towards what you need and want to experience or achieve the most.

For me, that is peace. Bravery is one of the things I must embody to keep my peace. As a result, it's how I earn respect for myself, which is something no one can take from me. I earned it, and am constantly earning to keep it. It's mine. It's what I have built my character from. And building your character is exactly what you're doing through this process of picking a CCT, holding it as the way for you to earn respect for yourself, and then working to earn and keep it.

Finally, I will leave you with this: Choose to be brave because you don't want to let fear keep you away from what is most precious to you, in every situation. Give yourself the chance to earn respect for yourself by building yourself into the person you really want to be. Just don't let the rats, black cats, and all their friends sabotage you, because nothing, and no one, has the right to do that to you.

To summarise the final chapter of the book:

 CCTs are the qualities that you consciously decide to embody, intentionally shaping the essence of who you are.

 It is ideal to have a framework to guide your choice of CCTs.

My personal framework is choosing them based upon my needs. So I pick traits based on what I have to be to fulfill my needs.

Fear has been a great interrupter in my need for peace.

Bravery is the conscious character trait I have chosen to embody, meeting my need for peace by facing and fighting my unhelpful fears.

Once a CCT is chosen, focus on nurturing and embodying it.

I do this by using my CCTs as the primary way I earn respect for myself.

Call to Action: Pick bravery as one of your CCTs, and do something, anything, this week that gives you the chance to earn it.

Conclusion

I wrote a book about the fear-facing journey because it was one of the most empowering things I did for myself. Living life without knowing exactly who you are and what's existing inside of you can be incredibly difficult. You feel lost and confused because you don't understand why you're making the decisions you are and why you're reacting the way you are. You feel out of control, because, in reality, you are out of control—of yourself.

That can change. And you are the one who can change it.

Imagine waking up one year in the future. You've just spent the past year thoroughly dedicating yourself to addressing all the things blocking you from experiencing life the way you want to. You faced your fears and dissipated them by changing your beliefs. You learned

about your needs and started to figure out ways to fulfill them. You connected better with people you love. You're in tune with your emotional state and are learning how to balance it. You are consciously reacting to situations and owning your responses.

You're not constantly and unhelpfully afraid anymore of the amplified things that used to torment and sabotage you. You're not being led by beliefs that are hurting you and immediately changing them instead. You're not living in the pain of extreme need deprivation. You're not being triggered with negative emotions everywhere you go anymore.

Instead, you are aware—of your thoughts and feelings. Your fears and beliefs. Your needs and powers. You are aware of what is positively and negatively affecting you in your environment and respond to them as such. You are aware of what is a true danger to you and what isn't. You wake up every morning with a clear mind. You quickly and effectively deal with any issues that arise. You are living better and happier.

I confidently say this is what is possible for you, because it's been my experience. The time it takes will be different for all, but this is the place I'm in right now. That's why my peace and happiness are what I value most in life. I worked extremely hard to earn them using this process, not knowing that they would be the gift I'd be receiving. They can be your gift, too, if you are ready to earn them with me.

Finally, to summarise *Facing Fear, Finding You*:

There are multiple forms of fears, with unconscious permanent internal fears (rats) being a danger to you. Amplified dangers (black cats) are those you fear that don't pose as severe a threat to you as you believe.

By taking safety from the presence of fears in your life, you have not only become comfortable with them, but are living through them. You can change this, one way being creating a conscious permanent internal fear of your rats.

You face your fears by looking closer at your blind spots (bs boxes). Begin by picking your greatest fear, and then identify the general danger that fear is related to.

Next, pull the general danger apart into specific situational fears (strands) to face all the ways you are afraid of the amplified danger. You can pull substrands also.

Focus on your responses to your rats. Freezing takes the form of your mind only focussing on the threat, nothing else, while also either going blank, catastrophising the danger, or knowing but not being able to take action. The belief of powerlessness is often the cause of your freeze response.

The running response is made of your actions to create distance between yourself, the rats, and the black cats. The first form of running is avoiding the danger, and the second is denying the existence of the fear and danger. The main reason people run is because they believe it's the only power they have.

Facing or exploring how fear is affecting you and what you believe are the consequences of the danger becoming a reality allows you to see and question those beliefs.

Beliefs are deeply ingrained convictions that take many forms. Negative beliefs (moths) hinder and harm you; positive beliefs are helpful.

There are many forms of power, with internal power being endless in its potential to take the form you need the most. You can earn internal powers by creating a conscious general positive belief (mother belief) of them and then using the power. Or you can use the power through fear, and the belief is formed naturally from the evidence you gain.

We all have physical and internal needs, and sometimes we fear the deprivation of our needs. That fear can be helpful; however, sometimes, we fear our internal needs themselves. These fears are rats and black cats.

A principle is a belief you consciously use to shape your decisions, actions, and reactions, intentionally optimising your experience of life. Conscious principles of life can be an excellent ally in your fight against fear. Living from principles of obligation, however, is not.

Conscious anger can be a powerful way to take yourself out of a debilitating fear response long enough to start thinking clearly. Our belief systems exist as an intricate maze, with our emotional triggers and actions being held in the set destinations our beliefs are leading us.

Conscious character traits are the qualities that you consciously decide to embody, intentionally shaping the essence of who you are. I choose them based upon my needs, and bravery is one I've chosen to embody, meeting my need of peace by facing and fighting my unhelpful fears.

Thank You

Thank you for sharing this journey through these pages. Your time and attention mean everything to me. If this book has resonated with you in any way, I'd be truly grateful if you'd consider leaving a review. Your words not only help other readers find their way here but also help me understand how these ideas have helped you. It would mean the world to me if you would leave a review on the platform where you bought my book, and share it with everyone you think it could help.

Thank you to all of my supporters on this journey. You know who you are.

For more insights, and to follow my author journey, visit: www.ikrandhawa.com.

Wishing you well, and I will see you in the next book.

Indi

Glossary

Rats - Unconscious permanent internal fears

Black Cats - Amplified dangers

Killer Comfort Blanket - Fearful comfort

General Danger - The general overarching danger you are afraid of, such as grief or intimacy

Strands of Fear - The specific situational fears that are attached to the general danger, such as the fear of a specific person passing away

The Residence - Your internal home environment

BS Boxes - Internal blind spots

Moths - Negative beliefs

Mother Belief - General conscious positive belief

Child/Children Beliefs - Situational conscious positive beliefs coming from the mother

The Maze - Made of walls of beliefs, leading your thoughts down set paths to the destination of emotional triggers and actions

CCTs - Conscious character traits

About the Author

I.K. Randhawa (pronounced I.K. Ran-dha-wa) is on a mission to guide those suffering from internal chaos and emotional overwhelm through deep internal exploration, so they can finally find peace, purpose, and personal freedom.

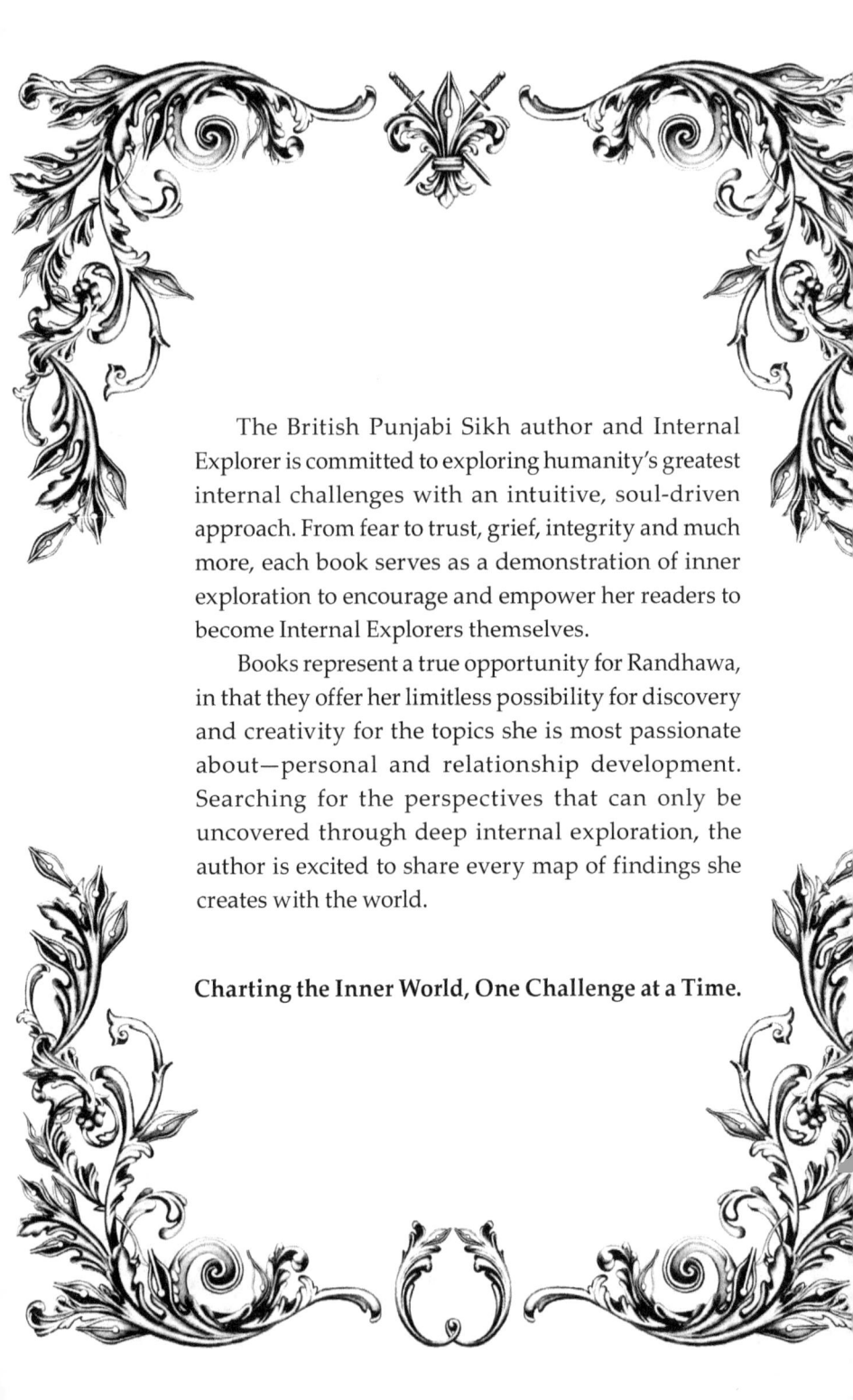

The British Punjabi Sikh author and Internal Explorer is committed to exploring humanity's greatest internal challenges with an intuitive, soul-driven approach. From fear to trust, grief, integrity and much more, each book serves as a demonstration of inner exploration to encourage and empower her readers to become Internal Explorers themselves.

Books represent a true opportunity for Randhawa, in that they offer her limitless possibility for discovery and creativity for the topics she is most passionate about—personal and relationship development. Searching for the perspectives that can only be uncovered through deep internal exploration, the author is excited to share every map of findings she creates with the world.

Charting the Inner World, One Challenge at a Time.